Lancashire Hotch Potch

"A Second Helping"

by
Kay Davenport

Also by Kay Davenport:
A LANCASHIRE HOTCH POTCH
SOME OLDHAM TIMES
MY PRESTON YESTERDAYS

In bookshops or from the author
(see inside back cover)

For ...
Anne, Hilary, Peter and Martin

©Kay Davenport 1991
C.I.P. A catalogue record for this book is available from The British Library.
ISBN 0 9514335 1 2 Lancashire Hotch Potch "A Second Helping." (Pbk).

Cover emblems designed by Alistair Brooks. Hop-Scotch drawing by R. Embleton.
Typeset and printed in England by Hirst, Kidd & Rennie Limited, Union Street, Oldham

Contents

7	1922 Guild Memories
8	Your Caring Sharing Co-op
12	A Preston Whit Monday
15	Lancashire Luxuries
18	Frenchwood, Preston
22	Lancaster Road, Preston
25	Our Gracie
27	The Brewery
38	Doin' My Front
41	Memories of a Winckle
46	Sixty Years On
50	The White Windsor Soap Works, Preston
54	The Home Fires
56	Monkey Runs
58	Generation Gap
60	Skeleton in the Cupboard
61	The Phantom
63	Magic!

4 LANCASHIRE HOTCH-POTCH

Samuel Smith's Brewery Workers, c.1880 (The Brewery)

HOUSE OF COMMONS
LONDON SW1A 0AA

FOREWORD

For many years Kay Davenport has delighted us with her writings of old customs, happenings and events, especially here in the North of England. This book, "A Lancashire Hotch Potch Second Helping" is no exception.

It is a joy to read, and it places on record, so much of our wonderful history, in real human terms.

I hope the book will be widely read, and I thank Kay for writing it, and giving so much pleasure to so many people.

SIR CYRIL SMITH   MBE DL
Member of Parliament

ACKNOWLEDGEMENTS

I would like to thank the kind correspondents who have shared their Lancashire memories with me in the past and for encouragement for the future. Also to my family and to all who have given me advice. I am very grateful to Sir Cyril Smith, MBE, DL, MP, for writing the foreword.

For use of photographs, I am indebted to the Lancashire Evening Post, Oldham Local Interest Centre, Saml. Smith's Brewery, The Co-operative Union and J. N. Nichols (Vimto) plc.

1922 Guild Memories

We Prestonians expect everyone else to know what the phrase 'Once every Preston Guild' means, for we know that the Guild occurs every twenty years, since the eleven hundreds. It is often used to denote the rarity of something happening ... say for example the time lapse between a husband remembering to buy his wife flowers, or some such treat. We older ones also know that we missed a Guild in 1942, being busy elsewhere than Preston, in fact our men and womenfolk, too, were scattered all over the place in what was euphemistically called the 'Theatre of War'. There are historical books detailing facts and figures of the famous Guilds, but some of my memories are personal, and some I have collected from others. To be able to see four Guilds means one has had a long life, and to be able to remember the first in one's life at three years old is good; from infanthood, to salad days, on to young wife-hood and widowhood, from being a howling child in a go-chair to a white-haired grandmother, a whole life-time which seems to have gone in a flash ... but now to earliest memories, the first one of an oft-told tale...

Both stories have sequels more than sixty years later...

At the time of the 1922 Guild Avenham Park was the venue for Preston schools' celebrations, one of which was a pageant featuring tableaux about our Commonwealth.

I was taken by my parents, I recall the details so clearly. I was in what was called a 'go-chair' and today would be called a 'baby buggy'. It had wooden handles, a wooden foot-rest, side-arms of wood, and was constructed of something like tapestry or carpetting. I know that I drummed my little feet in their small boots on the foot-rest and screamed in terror at what was, to me, a very large and menacing furry growling brown bear. As it looked above me, cavorting, Father told me it was 'Just a man in a skin'. I refused to believe this and had to be taken home howling, whilst my elder sister was furious because she had to go home, too.

Sixty years later, after I had an article published in the Lancashire Evening Post, their diarist uncovered a programme of the Guild which showed that St. Luke's School had a tableau of Canada with Red Indians, fishermen, lumberjacks ... and a bear whose name in the cast list was 'A. G. Fry'.

Several ladies wrote to me saying that the said 'bear' had 'led them a dog's life' as it was a naughty lad in a skin who terrorised them with his antics! He certainly petrified my small three-year-old self, and was never to be forgotten. I must have been easily scared in 1922 for my father, who worked for the 'Post', appeared as an apprentice of Caxton, in a tableau upon a flat horse-drawn cart.

He had a small dress-rehearsal for this, and Mother and I were treated to the sight of him in a ratty wig, a full beard and dressed in a tunic and baggy tights. He looked so bizarre to me, as he was normally bald-headed and with a russet moustache. I can recall so vividly leaping up and down like a dervish on our horse-hair sofa, once again screaming blue-murder till he returned to normality.

On giving a talk in 1990 at Sharoe Green Hospital, I was shown an actual 1922 copy of what was then 'The Lancashire Daily Post'. It was yellow and crumbling (just like I feel on a bad day!) and, pictured in this newspaper, was my father, just as I had remembered him and as he had terrorised me almost as much as that blessed bear of so very long ago. Now, an elderly lady, I had to struggle with the threatened tears. Strangely enough, a gentle patient in the audience, who was not too sure of the happenings of the present time, could clearly remember the 'Bear' who was A. G. Fry, as she had attended the same school in 1922.

Preston ladies have written to me telling of how they were shepherdesses in the 1922 Guild, again on Avenham Park. I can tell them what they wore and what they carried then. They remember the pleasure of being young and dancing on the grass, lovely things to recall when one is over seventy years old. I know that they carried white crooks, trimmed with ribbons. I even know that the wood of those crooks had a harsh feel, and experience tells me that they must have been painted with emulsion paint ... and not gloss! My sister's shepherdess's crook stood a long time in the corner of our living room alongside the umbrellas and Grandad Williams's night-stick from his police days. In the twenties, folk in small houses such as ours did not often possess a hall-stand. (I know a man whose earliest memories of a 'corner' held his grandad's wooden leg a mememto of the first war and his dad's rifle from the 1939 war when home on leave ... what a sad vignette).

The 1922 shepherdesses bring to mind a far prettier picture in their quilted lavender-coloured skirts and pink frilled jackets and be-ribboned poke-bonnets. Treasured memories for many an old Prestonian who may, with luck, see their fourth Preston Guild.

On a far grander scale, and sure to be in pictures of the '22 Guild, Mrs. Astley-Bell, the Guild Mayoress, wore a magnificent ball gown which is valued and owned to this day by Mrs. Grayling of Garstang, who is her daughter.

One of my kind correspondents, Mrs. Edna Cattermole, of New Longton, tells me that her uncle, who had a bicycle repair shop and who was the proud owner of a black Ford car with a canvas hood, called a Tin Lizzy, gave a family treat in the '22 Guild remembered to this day. Uncle hired a room over a bicycle shop at the top of North Road, packed picnic baskets for the family, who then lived on a farm at Goosnargh, and they were all thrilled by the torchlight procession as it wound its way through the lamp-lighted streets of the town. There were costumed walkers representing folk from all the countries of the world carrying lighted torches ... 'Marvellous', recalls Mrs. Cattermole, as no doubt do other Prestonians lucky enough to be alive at this time. Mrs. Cattermole also remembers that one family party walked all the way from Blackburn with baskets of food for one of the Guild days in 1922!

An old friend of my uncle's remembers that he and other lads from his church, St. Joseph's, had to walk on one procession carrying a lily each. They were all representing angels ... It's hard to imagine today's street-wise boys agreeing to do this in 1992; certainly there would be some unangelic language if it were even suggested!

Recently, whilst addressing a T.G.W. meeting in Rochdale, and mentioning Preston Guild, an old lady was delighted to tell me that she attended Eldon Street School in 1922 and was 'Polly Put the Kettle On' in the Nursery Rhyme contribution to the Schools' effort. She insisted on having her kettle full of water, refusing to take part unless she could have this. She remembers tripping up over a tuft of grass and losing the water. Just a little thing to remember, but a precious recollection.

When one is elderly, youthful happenings of seventy years ago often come to the surface of the mind in old age ... the lovely ones are the jewels to be looked at and treasured, as I well know.

Your Caring Sharing Co-op

At the time of the 1922 Guild, the Co-operative Society was playing quite a big part in the lives of Lancashire people.

An advertisement in the Lancashire Daily Post (as it was called then) proudly proclaimed their progress since the Guild of 1902.

There had been an increase in membership from 12,831 to 35,300. Their capital had increased from £126,093 to £630,209. They had reserves, increased from £5,268 to £88,458. Furthermore, £1,713,308 had been paid out as 'Divi' on purchases and interest since the previous Preston Guild of 1902. Considering that a large loaf cost fourpence in 1922, the Co-op had justification in blowing its own trumpet.

Many a 'Potato-lad' who started with the Co-operative movement rose to be managers in time and I have had many little anecdotes passed on to me, and many little tales have winged their way down the years to this time of the 1992 Guild ... little snippets, one might say, of local and co-operative folklore. Grandmas and grandads, some long gone, have contributed, along with personal memories, to this hotch potch of Lancashire Co-op history...

Looking at today's Superstores and Co-op Shopping Giants, where floors are often carpeted, it is difficult to visualise that the Co-op shops had flagged or wooden floors, and that children who made too much clatter with their clogs were severely frowned upon by the 'store' manager. Today, some of those same shops in Lancashire are transformed into Hindu Temples, Mosques or Islamic Teaching Centres. The Koran will be chanted where once Lancashire mothers shopped for black puddings, bacon or potatoes.

A young lad in the twenties or thirties, being employed by the Co-ops of the times, was said to have landed 'A reet good job'. Industrious little fellows could progress to being the 'flour lad' or even having charge of the bacon counter, then often to being manager. The first two jobs were carried out in the back shop. There, the potato lad weighed out potatoes as they thundered down the big chute from an upstairs room. He had to take care not to mix up his King Edwards with his Jersey spuds. He sometimes permitted a new mother to weigh her bundled-up new baby in the scoop of the scales in the days before there were proper clinics.

The shop windows were packed solid with imitation kegs of butter, great blocks of lard, and sacks of sugar or flour. When a new cereal called 'Force' appeared, packets of this would be piled up high in the window and there would be brightly coloured pictures of 'Sunny Jim', an odd-looking character with a pig-tail, and the caption read ... 'High O'er the fence leaps Sunny Jim, Force is the power that raises him'. The breakfast food was supposed to give him boundless energy! Sunny Jim featured often in the Oxford Street Co-op in the 30's.

A Prestonian who was a 'Potato Lad' in the early thirties remembers when in his day 'Hygiene and Safety Acts' were being introduced, shop assistants were encouraged to wash their hands more often. One dinner-time the small lad was left in charge at the Co-op counter and he had to go out to the W.C. in the yard. An impatient customer, a dragon of an old lady, was waiting.

'Weer's ta bin?' she asked, and on being told she demanded, 'All lady-like', that the little fellow washed his hands. 'Na then ... that's better', she said, so the young assistant told her ... 'Right, Mrs. Smith ... I've washed my hands, what can I get you?'

'Two bundles o' firewood and a packet o' firelighters', she demanded, nose in the air!

Another 'Co-op story' is remembered by my sister-in-law, who worked for the Co-op. During the war, when there was a paper shortage, toilet rolls went up in price from fourpence-halfpenny to sixpence. A customer, expecting visitors, asked the price, having only fivepence in her hand. On being told, apologetically, by Alice of the higher price, the disappointed woman said ... 'Never mind, I'll have a couple o' pan-shiners instead!'

Alice also recalls working in an Oldham co-op and weighing out meticulously small amounts of plug tobacco for pipe-smoking. If she got it wrong at the first cutting, and had to add a sliver more of the strong-smelling stuff, the tiny addition was placed on top of the plug and called 'a jockey'.

Small bags were not used for ounces of pepper or spice, but little cones of paper had to be twisted around and the little end secured at the bottom so that nothing was spilled. Quite an art, not one a present-day assistant would take to kindly ... and in any case, who would have the time for such niceties now?

There were no electronic check-outs in the twenties or thirties, instead many shops had cash-desks where the cashier ensconsed on a high stool, had a clear view of the shop. This was usually a lady, in a high-necked blouse and long skirt. Money was placed in a brass cup and sent winging along on overhead wires by means of a little pulley from assistant to cashier. In a Preston Broadgate shop, the lady was much admired by an assistant who did indeed become the shop's manager.

Daily, he would place a silver-paper-wrapped chocolate in the little money-cup and send it shooting along to his lady-love. You can't send tokens of affection on an electronic till, can you? (One naughty flour-lad once wrapped up a cow's eye from the butcher's and sent that on its overhead journey to the cash-desk lady. Another Preston assistant made up a 'box of chocs' with silver-paper-wrapped sheep's eyes!!). There were no security systems, either, and in that same shop there was a mystery surrounding the custard tarts. These kept disappearing from the counter as if by magic and no-one could guess how they went A.W.O.L. A bright assistant thought he had the answer, and who the guilty party was. As he served this well-dressed customer one morning, in an excess of enthusiasm, he leaned across the counter, grasped her strongly by the fore-arms, crying heartily ... 'And how ar'ta today, Mrs. T?' She had wide fur-trimmed sleeves to her winter coat and, as the assistant squeezed, a turgid stream of bright yellow custard oozed slowly out of her cuffs and over her pudgy hands. Was HER face red! Another customer took her scissors along when shopping at the Co-op. Sausages, linked and hanging up, were snipped off to drop into her carpet bag, as her husband occupied the attention of the assistant.

On a more sombre note, a friend's uncle was a funeral director for the Co-op during the war. Two sisters, one very deaf, had gone to make arrangements for a third sister's burial. The director asked if they wanted grass mats provided as the ground was muddy. The deaf sister was puzzled by this and kept asking why these were necessary. Patiently, it was explained, and all thought she understood. As they left, she said loudly ... 'But why do we need our gas masks for a funeral?' This was, of course, in the days when it was obligatory for us to carry such horrors as masks.

Most Co-op members used their funeral services, and an Oldhamer tells me that at his store 'Divi' was given if mourners also had their 'Funeral Party' at the Co-op cafe. (I remember a southerner, long ago, visiting the north, was amused by notices in cafes stating 'Funeral Parties Catered For'. She thought the idea of a 'Party' at such times very strange!).

I remember that when there was a death in our family Mother would unearth a little 'Burial Pay-In book', take it along to Lancaster Road Main Co-op Office and go shopping. I recall her looking unusually smart at one such time in a skunk-trimmed black velour coat, high-domed black hat and new black strapped shoes and black stockings. The few pounds paid out at such times seemed to cover for such contingencies as well as a funeral. A collector came for the odd pennies each week for the club, so that the worry of paying for a funeral and mourning clothes was taken away. (In the seventies, a friend told me she claimed from a burial club which had been paid up long ago, and Eight Pounds was recovered ... not much use these days!).

I do remember myself that, in the thirties, some people still wore black for six months following a family bereavement, then purple or lavender clothes were considered 'proper'.

There was not so much reticence in discussing death then as now. During the war, in a pub kitchen where women used to gather, funeral arrangements were being discussed. Some were discussing family plots and where they themselves would finally rest. One spinster was saying she did not have a family grave to look forward to. 'Never mind, Florrie', said a kindly neighbour, 'Y'a can come in wi' me, there'll be room fer one on top!' Apparently, one grave had space for six, which seems rather excessive, so I could be wrong!). As I had just travelled from Manchester to Oldham on a tram that evening, and the conductor had called out ... 'Full up inside, room on top', this struck me as rather bizarre at the time. Funny how things can stick in the mind for almost half a century!

I have also been told that there was a non-contributory burial scheme, the pay-out depending upon how much was spent at the Co-op in the quarter or so before the cash became needed. Should an unhappy lady be observed spending more than usual at the 'store' and her husband was known to be 'proper poorly', her shopping cronies would lower their eyes and murmur to each other that 'so and so' had not long to live. The poor lady was not so much as stocking up her cupboards for a rainy day as helping to obtain a little dignity of a decent burial for someone who may have worked very hard to obtain just a meagre standard of living. Such a sad little story encapsulates the pathetic poverty of the Lancashire of the past ... when 'Britain's Bread Hangs By Lancashire's Thread', or so we were told ... and a fat lot of good it did many of us.

Of course, we must remember that life is made up of sunshine and shadows, better perhaps to recall the stories which make us happy.

On a more cheerful note, another Preston gentleman in his seventies wrote and told me of 'Magical days' when Co-op field days were regular events in the town's calendar.

The 'Co-op Field Days' were always on a Saturday in early June, when any poor child between the ages of five and fourteen had to report to the shop at a given time. Boys had to have a tin mug tied to their braces with string, little girls had theirs fastened to their sashes or belts. 'Best' clothes would be worn but, sad to remember, many were clad in hand-me-downs, and clogs or boots were pathetically worn, irons missing from clogs, and little boots or shoes down-at-heel. Shame-faced small fellows often had their heads shaved because they had suffered from nits ... a short tuft of hair was left at the front ... handy for any short-tempered teacher to tug! Little girls might be lucky to have ribbons in their hair ... others had to make do with a torn-off strip of bright cotton cloth. Brave attempts to 'keep up appearances' were made in those days when there was very little to spare for 'dressing up' ... or any dress at all, for that matter.

But we are all recalling a day of excitement and delight, for on such a day each shop had its own band to play the children to the parks or to Preston North End's ground. The sound of the music floated into the air all over the town ... magical. In lines, laughing and singing to the music, the little children marched or danced along in holiday mood.

Mothers and fathers, grandmas and grandads met the youngsters at the parks ... then the picnic was served. My old gentleman remembers that gallons of coffee, and thousands of Bath buns, were consumed ... nobody went hungry on that day, and parents were happy to know that for once their children had full stomachs.

There were stunt men, jugglers, men on stilts and, best of all, the clowns. Girls took along clothes lines for skipping to the music ... 'All in together girls, very fine weather girls ... O.U.T. spells OUT!' Does anyone, besides me, remember such rhymes? Another puzzling one was chanted as a ball was bounced ... 'One, two, three allaira' ... whatever could that have meant? Such rhymes in bright young voices much have filled the air on Co-op field days long gone.

More than half a century later, my correspondent, Mr. Kelly, treasures this memory.

Modern children would be amazed at the little embarrassments which could be suffered by those on the poverty line during the depression. Jam jars would be taken back to shops for the halfpenny given and cash coupons for coppers were enclosed with certain packets of tea in Preston. Little kids would have to trudge to Bamber's Yard where the office was in order to get the hand-out in Preston. (I know, for I was there!).

Quarter-day was eagerly awaited when the pay-out (sometimes as much as 2/6d in the pound) was given to prudent housewives who had been sticking little yellow strips of those checks on to gummed sheets, with many a lick of the fingers as well as many an adding up of the amounts. First the mother would add up, and then the father would do it again ... just to make sure.

Mothers used to go to the main office of the Co-op in Lancaster Road if they wished to cash in their Co-op checks before quarter-day. A little less divi was paid out for this concession, which was often necessary to meet an unexpected bill. One old friend remembers how her grandmother's false teeth had to paid for in this way. Also, in those days, shops displayed little notices ... 'Please DO NOT ask for Credit, as a REFUSAL often offends'.

The other day, in a Co-op Superstore, the pop song blaring forth was ... 'I WANT it all, I want it NOW'. It made me think ...

Credit was certainly not allowed for any coal bill then, a mother had often to wait for the father to come home with his wage packet so that the bill could be paid. Then the family awaited anxiously for the clop of the coal-cart horse's hooves, knowing that there would be coal for the hearth which had been swept free of ashes. Then life could return to the living-kitchen, for the fire was the centre of domesticity then, being the only warm spot in a house of those times.

In Preston, just as certain shops had to be patronised for Whitsuntide finery for the Sunday School processions, so had certain shops to be used to stock school uniforms should a child be fortunate enough to be allowed to attend a Grammar School. I say 'allowed', for many a child, even though the scholarship be obtained, had to go to work in the mill instead.

The lucky ones often purchased their new school clothes at the Co-op, in the 'Mantle Department', which was also in Lancaster Road or Ormskirk Road around the corner. Because of the 'divi' many a Park School Girl or Grammar School boy was fitted out there. Sometimes the serge of the gymslip or the nap on the blazer might not be of the highest quality, but the Co-op knew its customers, and how to keep costs as low as possible, for folk who had to look twice at every penny before spending.

Yes, the Co-op must be remembered today by many a pensioner, for it played a big part in the lives of so many of us, in the days when we were young.

Most Lancashire towns had Clog Funds, set up to provide warm, almost everlasting clogs, clogs which 'grew' with the child because of the skill of the cloggers of the times. Necessity really was the mother of invention in this case.

I am indebted to an Oldham pensioner for the following ... This man, when a small poor boy, had to go to the King Street Co-op cloggers' shop for the clogs supplied by the Education Committee to hundreds of little lasses and lads of those awful poverty-stricken times. When the right size was found, allowing plenty of room for growth, the clogger took a branding tool and a hammer and the words 'Oldham Education Committee' was imprinted deep enough 'to be seen a mile off'. This was so that the clogs could not be pawned. Apparently, the clogs were almost everlasting for, as the feet grew, the old clog sole was discarded and a leather toe-cap was added to the uppers and then a new wooden sole fitted. It is no wonder such an experience for a sensitive child can haunt an old person today ... a memory of those famous 'Good Old Days!' Like the words on the sole, indelibly branded.

My mother never would let me have clogs, though I longed to be able to make sparks on the flagstones as some of my little pals did. It was Mother's proud boast ... 'You never wore clogs', as though that were proof-positive that we always 'kept our heads above water', though I must say we often were in fear of sinking a bit, as were so many families in those times in Preston, or anywhere else for that matter.

A personal Preston memory of when I worked in Stoneygate Nursery School, that haven for many a poor little soul in the 30's, we provided little clogs for children who did sometimes come practically barefoot to school. (I recall one little chap, legs bowed like bananas from rickets, once attending with his mother's white, down-at-heel dirty-white court shoes on ... I even remember his name, I hope he lived to wear Gucci boots.

Another little Stoneygate memory surfaced recently when I was buying Lychees to put in a fresh fruit salad. They cost 95 pence for half a pound ... roughly twice the amount I got for a week's work when I was an assistant earning 10 shillings a week (less 7 pence stamp) in Preston when I was seventeen. A little boy called Gerry, who was a twin and is perhaps a grandfather, now brought me some Lychee nuts as a present from his dad, who was in the merchant navy. I ate them as I watched over the class of toddlers as they took their lunchtime nap on their little truckle beds. I remember thinking, as I ate the luscious scented fruit, what a contrast it was to the experience of sitting there next to my little charges who so often smelled of warm, wet knickers or the aroma of their little broken-down shoes and holey socks of some of the little mites who enjoyed the care of Stoneygate staff.

Gerry had a lisp and he kept telling me he now had a 'new tailor toot' and I was ages in finding out (much to his frustration) that he was the proud possessor of a new sailor suit! I wonder if Gerry still remembers it as I do?

A Preston Whit Monday

As Sunday School scholars in the thirties, as Whitsuntide drew near, we were all reminded that it was the time when we had to 'Stand up for Jesus'. In other words, we had to bear witness, and march in the processions of witness.

I'm sorry to remember that we little Protestants (or Prodidogs, as we were sometimes called) didn't worry too much if the rain came down on the Orangemen or the Catholics (or Catlicks — we retaliated) so long as the sun shone on OUR parade! Even the smallest among us had to 'walk' as a declaration of faith, although we still had a lot to learn about hope, and that other most important of virtues ... charity. We were children, and therefore we thought as children, so were not TOO concerned if a downpour of rain in the morning darkened the gaudy suit of William of Orange astride his white horse (which was on loan from the milkman). The royal hat with its many plumes might become a sorry sight with the feathers all uncurled by the rain.

We were not too sympathetic, either, if the ladies in the Catholic procession, which followed next, had their biblical raiment streaked with rain. The make-up of the holy women and saints often got badly smudged, and heavily applied lipstick and eyebrow pencil looked grotesque when running down powdered faces. Crepe whiskers and beards did not take kindly to the soaking which they sometimes got from the unkind weather at many a Whitsuntide remembered. (In any case, Mother thought the Virgin Marys, even though they were in tableaux, looked improper wearing lipstick ... though it was all right for Mary Magdalen ... Mother said!).

The elaborate scenes from the Bible, displayed on flat-top carts pulled by straining horses, or sometimes by lines of youths, could look pathetic after a heavy downpour. Parents would worry, too, about the ruination of dearly-bought new clothes. In the days before my time, we are told that Whit finery often was destined for the pawn shop. (That must have been in those infamous 'Good Old Days'). Meanwhile, and back in the days of the thirties, we children watching the others, safe and dry under our umbrellas, prayed that the rain would cease for us in the afternoon, when it was our turn; and for other smaller denominations.

On the evening before the Whit walks, the pavement along the route in Preston would be lined two and three deep with orange boxes, three-legged stools, spindle-back chairs and wooden forms. (In those days some families with many children used forms as seating at the table (a friend now in her seventies, recalls that in her large family of eight children, only the boys were seated at the table, the girls stood, there being no room for them!).

The pieces of poor furniture were left in place overnight, to ensure that their owners got a good view of the day-long processions. Should the evening before the walks be warm, the owners took advantage of this, and little groups of people sat and chatted together, sometimes sharing a bottle or two and many a joke and song. It was so important for mothers and fathers to get a good view of their children, especially as the clothes worn, the flowers carried and the new shoes and socks had been saved for in coppers over the year. Folk had to patronise certain shops, and little folk who might hardly have a Sunday frock or suit to call their own during the rest of the year, might be decked out like little royal children for this special time.

Parents and Grandparents made a show of running into the procession to hand pennies to the children, often to the horror of mounted policemen and watchers as police horses were startled by dashing careless donors. Many children were limping before the walk was over, for new patent-leather shoes or unyielding lace-up boots played havoc with tender little feet, and more blisters than banners would be raised on the day.

As children, watching on Church Street in the early morning, we were not interested in the Orangemen, though we were impressed by their Prince William in all his finery astride the great horse. Most Lancashire towns had a large contingent of Irish, and they marched along to bands playing strictly Irish music. We really were more interested in the Catholic processions, for their beauty.

The many tableaux were like pages from an illustrated Bible.

Scholars took on the mantles of saints or angels, and many a lad noted for his villainy would have the grace to look shame-faced as he portrayed a holy man or disciple. Especially would he look embarrassed if his pals of another faith would call out unkind things ... such as 'I like y'r frock, Bert', or 'Y'r wings are crooked, Tom', and the saint-for-the-day would wish himself elsewhere. Red-faced men, more used to flat caps, Woodbines and whippets looked mighty strange when sporting golden haloes and satin robes. Virgins-for-the-day tried not to look abashed when naughty bystanders passed comment. (Pubs often flouted the law and stayed open all day ... thus fuelling the rivalry). The butcher's boy might be Thomas the Doubter in tableau, asking to see the Lord's stigmata. The pert shop-girl could be Joan of Arc about to be burnt alive at the stake. All were silent actors elevated or beautified for just the one day. No wonder the priests and vicars hoped their several prayers for fine weather would be answered.

In among the winding long ribbon of spectacular brightness and glamour were the more sedate colours worn by the soberly-suited men of the bible classes and the carefully-stepping members of the Mothers' Unions. Faithfully, and sometimes painfully, in new shoes, they marched to support their Church and Sunday School. Mother walked as a member of her Union, but was cross because the Vicar's sister, who was a spinster, led her little band as President. (How could she know about being a Mother was the complaint — or about Union either, for that matter ... though this was said sotto voce in case any little big-ears were listening!). We usually were!

Some of the tots who had been kept in straight lines by their garlanded ropes and their teachers often fell by the wayside and had to be collected by parents. The scent of flowers mingled with the smell of manure from the many horses which drew the carts, and the terrifying police-horses which sometimes reared up if a loud band passed too close. Such horses could strike terror into little children, even those watching, for emotions could be easily stirred by the high sweet note of a trumpet, playing a well-known hymn, and unexpected tears flowed easily. The thump of a big bass drum could set the heart beating strongly, too.

Many an old eye would mist over at the sight of columns of white-clad and white shod little lads struggling by, flagging under the strain. The little hands, scrubbed clean for the occasion, were more used to clutching conkers and catapults than the pink carnations, or lilies, which were wired to stay upright. From the tops of the boys' heads, with hair 'powed' to basin-cropped neatness to feet uncomfortable in the shoes rather than the clogs and grey woollen stockings of everyday, they did not look QUITE at ease.

The great coloured banners, some garishly painted and with many coats of shining varnish, were most impressive. Should the day be windy, the carriers of the banners, in spite of the 'holders down', had a terrible battle to keep them aloft. For a blustery wind would fill them out like great sails and, like sails, they would hit the deck ... in this case the setts of the roads and streets of the route. On a particularly bad stretch, on a windy day, the poor men, uniformly dressed in their peaked caps and alpaca coats, would grow purple in the face and stagger hither and yon. Unkind people who didn't know better may have thought them drunk, so erratic was their progress. Bravely they struggled on, heroes to a man. Outside the Prison at Stanley Street, many a banner met its fate and seven or more would be flat on the pavement.

How men had striven, in relays, for the massive wooden poles which held the banners were terribly heavy, and changing of bearers was a tricky business whether it was windy or not, the leather holsters proving intractable more often than not.

I vividly remember one day of high wind. The banner near to which I was marching depicted our Vicar's father, The Rev. Barton Spencer, who had been the incumbent before him. His full portrait, bearded in clerical raiment, frighteningly fierce and forbidding, got a gale force wind behind it. Grimly, the men fought to keep their banner high and the painted face and flowing black vestments bellied out and back with a sick-making movement, the heaving vicar was too much for me, and I had to retire for a while, sick as a dog.

It was no wonder the public houses did a brisk trade. Many a Catholic 'angel' relieved of wings and halo at dinner time was glad to pull on his jumper and jacket and corduroys and head for the handiest hostelry. We younger ones were grateful for the tea and buns waiting for us in the schoolroom. The older folk who were unable to tackle the long walk had this little treat ready for us. The walking wounded were treated, too, and there was a great sense of relief all round.

It had been a long afternoon for us, from the assembly, the raising aloft of the great painted banners, the blessing before march-off to 'Onward Christian Soldiers' to the final 'Abide with Me' at the close. We all had felt to be a small part of a greater glory. We had been united, people of all ages and social standing. Some may have been cajoled into taking part, but most supported their church because their religion was an integral part of their lives, instilled at home and further strengthened by Church or Sunday School. We had to strive, however falteringly and often with many side-steppings, to follow the simple dictum of loving our neighbours.

Last year I stood in the cobbled street where we assembled more than half a century ago. The school against whose walls the proud banners of St. James's Church had rested before the march-off for the procession is now demolished.

It is difficult to recall that the church was so full each Sunday evening that forms had to be brought in for the overflow of people unable to find pews.

There will be many older people, like me, who recall the words of the Bishop of Blackburn in a confirmation address, when he used as his text ... **'Ye Shall be Witnesses unto me'.** At Whitsuntide so long ago, we hoped that this we had done with faith.

Lancashire Luxuries

To an elderly Lancashire friend of mine, luxury would have been a dry towel; I nearly said a dry bath towel, but to suggest that bath towels were usual in working class homes in the twenties would be wrong. Towels were nearly always white or cream, perhaps with a stripe down the middle, in red. There was usually a roller towel behind the back door in the kitchen for bathrooms were not commonplace, either, in those days.

This friend was the youngest of eight children and, as a child and because he was the last to get his Friday night bath, the few towels the family possessed were sopping wet when it came to his turn. Now that he can afford large fluffy bath towels, he luxuriates in their possession.

Of course, he never got clean bath water, either, for he was a child in the days when the tin bath was brought into the kitchen from the back yard, where it hung on a great nail. The eight children, in turn, got rubbed down with a soapy flannel and their hair washed with a block of hard soap ... no such luxury as shampoo for them. It was later when we were told by the power of advertising that 'Friday night is Amami night'. Then the flappers of those days were introduced to shampoos as well as powders and 'Snowfire' and 'Pond's' creams. How we hoarded our pennies for such exotic treats, often frowned upon by our parents! No, my old friend remembered only the scummy bath-water in the zinc tub, the sodden towels, and the strong soap which made the eyes run; no wonder he later appreciated a wallow in a bath with hot, scented water, and the delight of being cossetted by the use of a fluffy warm towel. You have to suffer the bitters to enjoy the sweets, as many an old Lancashire woman has suggested to her children.

My own personal luxury, and one which I longed for as a child, was to be able to get out of bed, put my feet upon a rug or carpet, and be able to go to the lavatory in the bathroom (when we moved from our terrace home to a semi) without touching any cold linoleum as I went.

My grandchildren would take it for granted that their feet are never frozen when in the house, but then, they haven't known the icy feel of linoleum on a cold morning, nor have they known how comforting could be the bliss of a home-made rag rug like a little island of comfort in a sea of icy lino to which the feet adhered, or even of varnished floorboards, such as many Lancashire people had in their terrace homes. As my mother would have said ... 'They don't know they're born!'

So now I doubly appreciate the comforts of a well-furnished house, a warm house, where children, if they so wish, can go barefoot and still be cosy. Our mothers would keep their hats on in the house on cold days, and have to keep to the one room for warmth ... 'Good old days? Not likely!

Other oldies of my acquaintance remember that on very cold winter nights, when icicles formed on the INSIDES of bedroom windows, that winter overcoats had to be placed on beds to supplement the inadequate blankets ... and this in the homes of working people, people who never knew what it was to have a day off and were lucky to have a holiday once a year, sometimes for just a day or two. Social History ... we Lancashire folk lived it, and the differences are incredible, and many youngsters must have difficulty in believing it. It is up to us older ones to keep them informed, for the changes in our lifetimes have been tremendous. We can read about Henry the Eighth in books, but we older men and women must record our own history, either by word of mouth or by writing it down. Some grandchildren will relish this ... others don't wish to know, but later on they may regret missing the chance to learn from those who have lived our Local Lancashire History.

A close friend of mine remembers what a thrill if was, when she began working just before the war, and was able to buy a 'costume' from a shop in Preston. She had an elder sister who was a 'costumier and dressmaker' and so all my friend's clothes had been home-made. The sister resented having to do this, for this brought no pay, meagre as it would have been, so the poor child was prodded with pins and had no say in the style or fit! The sister, in irritation, hurried the 'fittings', whizzing the poor kid about in the process. Beryl even remembers that some coats were made from bigger coats which had grown shabby, and the material turned so that there was a little 'pile' in the cloth and therefore looked nearer to a new garment. (I can imagine what our grandchildren would make of such stringencies today) for they are force-fed with teenage fashions on TV whilst still at school.

When Beryl was seventeen, the year Preston North End won the cup in 1938 and the game was being relayed on the wireless, she was setting out for the shops. She remembers that her Dad caller her back, for Mutch was about to take the penalty which secured the FA Cup. The town of Preston was in jubilant mood and she'll never forget the day when she bought her first costume ... costing two guineas ... luxury indeed!

Another old friend recalls how she hated a hand-me-down coat, so she looked for a telegraph pole which had been newly tarred so far up its length, and, as she said to me, 'she Clipped it up' ... meaning she put her arms around it as one would embrace a person, the coat was ruined, she got a smacking, but at least she got rid of the hated coat! When things were not so tight in Lancashire, my husband would joke about 'saving candle-ends' if I economised, and it seems that people did indeed save them, to be melted down and formed around a piece of string to make another candle. I'm assured that this was so, by folk today, who themselves can hardly believe that such economies were made.

Later on, during the war, when cosmetics were scarce, I certainly remember melting down lipstick ends, in an old large spoon, over a gas-jet, to pour the red liquid into a metal lipstick-case. Indeed, some of the 'cases' were made as 'foreigners' at munition works, as were little lighter-cases. A better use by far than making shell-casings and death dealing objects. Not that we thought that way then, as our saucepans and iron railings and even wedding rings were sacrificed for the war effort. Even a wedding ring was a Lancashire luxury for some women, if we are to believe that some poor souls had to make do with a curtain ring till finances improved.

Grandchildren may laugh when we cut the buttons from garments, to save them in a well-filled button box, the contents themselves being of historic interest to us older ones. The children are amused by buttons that graced their own 'rompers' or white pearl buttons that were cut from 'cami-knickers' worn by some of us during the war. (Very draughty ... and the buttons were always coming undone!) They themselves will have no such trivial mementoes, for they do not see the need to save buttons — they have the money for new ones. What were, and are, luxuries to us are taken for granted by modern children and their mothers ... lucky, lucky people!

It was considered a luxury to have one's shoes repaired by a proper cobbler who was often a clogger, too. When we were small, in the twenties, my father repaired all our shoes. He had a heavy last, bought the leather on Preston's flagged market, soaked it overnight, hammered it out and cut out the soles with the help of a paper pattern. He added soap flakes to the water, but he was impatient, and often the leather was not soaked long enough and had not enough 'give' in it. Then the toe would part company with the sole and I often had shoes with gaping fronts. They looked just like the mouths of voracious pikes with little brass brads like sharp teeth which cut into my tender toes so that sometimes they bled. I can see my Dad now, belting the soles with his hammer, holding the tiny brass nails in his mouth and, as he had a moustache resembling a russet hand-brush, the brads often got lost in the growth of his top lip. If he hit his nail with the hammer he would shout 'Cussit' or 'Hangmet' (whatever that meant), for swearing was not allowed in our home. When my elder brother 'tried it on' by singing a Stanley Holloway tune of the times about Anne Boleyn ... 'with 'er 'ed tucked underneath 'er arm, she walked the BLOODY Tower', he got a thick ear for his pains. Dad would be proud of the finishing repaired shoe and he would rub some heel-ball around the edges of the sole, and use a burnishing hammer as a final touch.

When he put 'Wood-Milne's' or 'Phillips' revolving rubber heels on his own shoes, the idea was that the heels were supposed to turn around as the heel wore down. How today's 'Doc Marten' shod children would hoot with laughter at this economy.

When my sister started work she took her shoes to the cobbler's little shop, which was also a 'cloggers', at the bottom end of Manchester Road. The shop was more like a hovel than anything else, with a most peculiar smell. It was very crowded because of the little iron mangle for pressing out leather and the festoons of clog-irons and trays of nails and pincers looking like torture instruments. We children had to sit on a wooden bench to wait, with many an ' 'Utch-up' to each other as more kids arrived to have irons put on their shabby clogs.

Because of the fire the tiny room was hot, and the odour from sweaty thick grey cycle stockings and old cut-down trousers and wet-sheep-smelling jerseys would be all pervading. The cobbler always needed a shave, he had blackened teeth and filthy fingernails. He wore a tatty leather apron, and his ancient mother crouched over the fireside. The floor was flagged, everything grimy. I hated going there and had to be bribed with tuppence by my sister. The Mother seemed to hate children, and as she frowned at us and spat in the fire, we thought she was a witch. (Elderly folk, sans teeth and often hairy-faced, wrinkled and yellowy, looked like witches then). Cobblers often sold cards of little metal segs, tiny half-moon shapes which had prongs underneath so that they could lengthen the life of a sole or heel. What pathetic economies we had to make then.

A friend whose father was a clogger told me that sometimes in the depression years a family would pay up for a repair with a bundle or two of firewood, and once with a tiny piglet. The piggy grew and couldn't be afforded, so had to be butchered. My friend recalled how the little kids of the neighbourhood gave the pig's head a kind of state funeral. They placed candles around it on the kitchen table, and solemnly paraded, singing a little hymn. When it became imperative that the head needed burial, the little kids crept out at dead of night and quickly interred it in the local park.

You don't get our highly automated shoe repairers getting such bizarre payment today, do you? No, materially at least, we are better off. It used to be clogs to clogs in three generations; now, in many cases (and many grandparents will see this now) it is a case of from clogs to skis in three generations … and good luck to them, say I.

And yet … and yet … because I myself try to encourage people of my age to remember what gave them pleasure in spite of poverty, there still was a sense of luxury, never to be forgotten in the feel of a flanelette nightie which had been warmed on the high, brass-edged fireguard. The remembrance, for the old ladies who were youngsters in the twenties, of newly-washed and sweet-smelling hair. Who could forget feeling fresh, clean and re-born on a Friday night after bath-time? How one's long hair was brushed and combed by a patient mother, who made ringlets by wrapping strands of hair into torn-off strips of shirt-laps? A girl-child had to hold on firmly to one end of the cotton or flannel strip whilst a mother did the twisting. Then the child could release her end of the rag at the crown and mother tied the ends together so that the result, next morning, was a riot of ringlets to delight the vanity of a growing girl. (Strange to tell modern little girls after watching 'soaps' such as 'Fame' or 'Neighbours' have pestered grannies today to tell them how to produce ringlets to ape the American or Australian child-actors! Old Lancashire grannies have had to rack their brains to recall how fancy ringlets were produced … as I know to my cost, not that there will be many flannel shirt-laps available today to be torn into strips!) Where, indeed, are COTTON shirt-laps?

Yet, bath nights, IF one got clean, warm water and a towel which had been warmed on the oven door, bare little bodies screened from the family by a clothes-maiden draped with a sheet to protect modesty (whatever happened to modesty?) may be 'remembered in tranquility' as just a little bit of simply luxury for some in the twenties or thirties. Then a child went off to a warm bed, a bed in which an iron baking-tray from the fireside oven had taken the chill off a bed in a cold unheated bedroom of the times. Even a housebrick could be made hot in the fireside oven and wrapped in a piece of flannel (another use for a shirt-lap) and placed in a chilly bed. Oh, yes — cosy, cheap luxury to delight a youngster then.

My friend, Rose, delights in buying the finest of fitted sheets, for she remembers the Lancashire habit of turning sheets 'sides to middle' when they became worn in the centre. It was a tricky task, for often the middles were so worn as to be almost threadbare (there must have been plenty of midfield confrontations to cause this!) I reminded Rose that during the last war, Queen Elizabeth, now the Queen Mother, was said to spend happy afternoons engaged in sewing the royal sheets in such a fashion on a royal sewing machine. (Surely the royal bedsheets didn't suffer the indignities as sheets from commoners' beds!) ... No matter, Rose now enjoys the comfort of sheets which are not lumpily seamed down the centre as, I trust, do our Royals ... but wartime, you see, was supposed to make commoners of us all, what with the mended sheets and the good King George the Sixth who decreed that we had only 5 inches of water in our wartime baths. How luxurious it is for us pensioners to be able to wallow in scented, foaming, CLEAN bathwater and to dry ourselves on the warm, dry towels, so appreciated when we recall our earlier times.

Finally, to amuse our young modern newly-weds ... I'll bet they don't have to furnish their front rooms with a large plant-stand topped by a spreading aspidistra in a big green plant-pot. They do not have to draw their lace curtains just so ... leaving a gap in order to display the plant to passers-by but not wide-open enough to show that the room is without furniture. This really was done in many a terrace home before the war, when folk furnished only the bare necessities ... bought with their own money, and saved for as a 'bottom drawer' before the wedding.

Sometimes Lancashire necessities were Lancashire luxuries.

Frenchwood, Preston

When I was a child in the twenties, fathers were the fount of all knowledge. I was told that the name Preston was derived from 'Priest's Town', that P.P. stood for Princeps Pacips which, Dad said, meant Prince of Peace, and when I attended the Park School in 1929 I was proud to wear the school badge on my blazer pocket, which showed the lamb and flag.

But Frenchwood? Dad could not tell me why the district north of the Ribble, the district where I spent my childhood, was so named.

There didn't seem much that was French about it ... true, there was Frenchwood House, just across 'the tip'. Had somebody called 'French' lived there? The only things French which we kids saw were the onion sellers with their strings of pinky-white onions tied to the handle-bars of their bicycles. The men wore dark berets, they spoke little English and they came in the same season every year to our house in Oxford Street, and Mother always bought from them. The straw strings of fat onions seemed faintly exotic in our little flagged pantry.

True, there were 'French' nuns who glided about the streets, on their way to Avenham Park, and Mother said some of them were holy ladies from a Carmelite Order which, she said, was French. They, too, seemed to belong to another world, and when the bells from St. Augustine's Church or the bell from the Larkhill Convent sounded and the day was bright and sunny, Frenchwood is remembered in the golden memory's eye of childhood as being faintly fantastical instead of plainly Lancashire.

In 1924 or thereabouts, there was a 'shower of frogs' in Selbourne Street ... Dad said they were French frogs, from across the Channel (a likely story!) and Mother said she had to go out with her yard-brush and sweep them into the gutter in the street ... I wonder if any old Prestonians remember that phenomenon?

When houses were built by the river near to Penwortham Bridge, the district was called 'The Boulevard'. That was deemed to be a 'new-fangled' French name, and though the term 'Yuppies' had not then been invented, some of the families of Frenchwood thought that folk were getting above themselves, and so were the builders to saddle solid Prestonians with fancy foreign-sounding addresses. We kids thought the name sounded 'posh'.

Of course, we had 'The Continental', which was a cafe along the river close to Broadgate, not far from our Frenchwood, where best-dressed Sunday strollers could partake of Vimto, or ice-cream served in little shell-shaped glasses. Visiting such a cafe, taking refreshment out-of-doors was as near as any of us came to a continental holiday then.

Before I was born, I am told by one old lady who lived next to the post office in Selbourne Street, opposite the convent wall, that there were fields with cows in them, a dairy where little children went with jugs to collect milk fresh from the cow. There was a joiner's shop, Mr. Simpson's, where little girls collected curling golden wooden shavings to tuck into bonnets to simulate ringlets. There was the 'Judge's House' at the top end of Selbourne Street, fenced off, with private fields filled with wild flowers, mayflowers, speedwells and daisies and clover ... remembered now by the lady now in her late eighties.

My own earliest memory of Selbourne Street in 1923 is of a long terrace of red-brick houses fronting on to a flagged pavement. Our house was in the middle of the row, facing where the Ribble Garage is now. There were flagged backyards to each house. The 'closet' whitewashed, and a coalhouse was in each yard. A neighbour hanged himself in his coalhouse, and Mother found him and ran out with her carving knife to ask a passing coalman to cut the poor fellow down. The man would not oblige, saying if it was God's will that the man hanged himself he would not interfere. Mother was desolate and today I remember the gloom which descended on our home. I was given a paint-box belonging to the unhappy fellow, which I treasured as a child.

It was a time of worry for many Lancashire folk, the depression was not too distant. We had knockers-up then, mill hooters going in the early morning, too. People kept pigeons and hens in their backyards; one man kept a pig in his.

Fathers were beginning to learn about cats' whisker wireless sets. I attended school at Grimshaw Street for the first time and I still remember that I forgot my lunchtime 'jam buttie' and that on the first day my sister and her friend made me walk behind them all the way. I actually recall walking on the rough ground and its cindery surface.

When she was a little girl at the beginning of the century, the area north of Selbourne Street was also known as 'The Tip', a black, cindery expanse where small children could dig up steel 'dobbers', those tiny spherical lumps of metal recovered from the slag dumped by foundries. There was so much dust about to plague the houseproud women when the weather was dry, so that the backs, those alleys behind their homes, had to be 'degged'. A degging can with a 'rose' was used to lay the dust ... especially on washing days, when each house had its own washing lines strung out and tied to the wooden clothes-posts. Should the coal man with horse and cart by imprudent enough to deliver on washing day, the housewife had to run out and prop up her lines with her longest clothes-prop so that the lumbering hourse could make way, with lowered head, underneath.

When it was bonfire night, the men of Frenchwood would collect skips from the mills nearby and, because these cane skips were oily, they burnt to a lovely silver filigree.

In summertime the long skipping ropes which were often the old and worn washing lines, were used for the games the bigger girls played. The dirt whipped up by the ropes made one cough so that it was not always easy to chant the rhymes of the times ... 'When I was in the kitchen, doin' a bit o' stitchin' ... in came a bogey man and knocked me out'. Many a pensioner of today must remember that. It was only later, when the streets were paved, that we could bounce our 'sorbo' balls and sing ... 'One, Two, Three, Allaira, I saw my Aunty Sara, Sitting on her BUMbalaira, eating ju-ju babies.' Then we could bowl our cane hoops, play at whip and top and battledore and shuttlecock. What innocent pleasure did the children of Frenchwood enjoy when that, as then unbuilt, area formed our playground.

The 'Tip', and later the allotments built on the lower grassy knoll fronting Frenchwood House, and where Frenchwood School stands now, were our happy hunting grounds as we made our own entertainment and played the games that children play ... or did!

In the 1920s the 'tip' was built upon, as was Frenchwood Knoll, so that some of the allotments were lost to the builders of some detached houses and many semis. What, in some ways, had been a quiet backwater was invaded by working-class folk wanting something a little better than backyards for their children to play in, though street games never lost their popularity when I was a child.

When the builders invaded, one of our favourite games was throwing half-bricks into the lime-pits, to watch them sink and churn up the sandy soil from below. The trick was to count how many you could lob in before the watchman chased you off!

Many a tradesman was able to manage the deposit or borrow it from a more affluent relation, and then the repayments would be found with many deprivations when the depression came along.

Hen-pens had to go, and I well remember that the man who kept a pig in his backyard in Selbourne Street was very unpopular. The neighbours got up a petition but my dad said he couldn't deprive a man of his livelihood, so he wouldn't sign. Mother was proud of him, but not the neighbours ... in any case, the poor pig had to go! And it did!

In 1926, because Mother could not settle in our house after the suicide and as the owner wanted it for himself, we had to move. So we moved just a few minutes walk away to the end of Oxford Street.

Strangely enough, it was a time for suicides in the next few years and they weighed very heavily upon me as a small girl.

Our coalman jumped from the Old Tram Bridge, or maybe he fell, leaving his flat cap on the boards. I don't know whether it was the same coalman who would not cut down the hanging man, I only know that our dog would never venture on the Tram Bridge. I had to carry him past the spot where the men went over, perhaps it was because the bridge was of wooden boards through which the water could be seen between the planks. I know it was difficult carrying a fat dog and wheeling my bike at the same time. As I passed the spot I always thought of the poor man's cap lying there.

A young man also hanged himself from the bannisters of his Frenchwood home when his parents were on holiday. On their return, and not being able to get into their house, a small friend was posted through the larder window and found the unhappy man. Three tragic deaths scar the mind when one is young and, of course, the dreadful times which Lancashire's unemployed had to endure may have contributed to the tragedies.

The times were a changing for Frenchwood. The Ribble Bus Company moved their works from Crown Street in 1927, and then the Offices from Lancaster Road were moved to Frenchwood. Leyland Lions and Tiger buses were built there, and when our roads were constructed, and tarmaccadam was laid over the black gritty thoroughfares, the chassis of the vehicles were tested upon them. The drivers manipulated the great steering wheels upon their long stems with their gauntletted hands. The men wore some sort of headgear with ear-flaps, and looked very high-up on their half-constructed buses.

The cost of the new roads fell upon the householders, which was quite a blow for some who were struggling, it was quite difficult for us, for we were on a corner, so had to pay for frontage in Oxford Street and also in Halsbury Street. The bill for one hundred and twenty pounds seemed tremendous, but I think arrangements were made for payment by instalments.

We got one small advantage from new road-building, for we kids were taken by our mothers (if we had a cold) to take big deep breaths at the side of the tar-wagons which were used in road-construction then. The fumes were supposed to 'clear our tubes'. Tar was quite a feature in our young lives; on hot days little balls of the stuff could be made by digging it up when it melted between the cobbles of our streets.

Our playing areas were getting smaller, but some of us were compensated for this by our moving into the new properties built by the Spencer family. (We kids thought they were very well-to-do, for Mrs. Rose Spencer always wore a new hat to church on Sunday, at St. James). There the histrionic vicar, a certain Lawrence Spencer, filled us with the fear of God each Sunday ... both morning and night of every sabbath.

So our families moved from terrace homes to semis, and we had gardens instead of backyards, halls instead of vestibules, and even porches. We learned to call our parlours lounges. We racked our names for house-names. My dad called ours Brooklyn, because there was a brook at the back of the houses at the park end of Selbourne Street (culverted now) and because my name was Kathlyn he added the 'lyn' to 'brook'. My friend Jess's parents called their house 'Hollywood' simply because there was holly in their garden. It seemed strange, really, for the two names sounded more American than English. Jess was my best friend when we were seven years old, and today, in 1991, we are still friends. Jess's mum was a darkly handsome woman, and one day as she stood at her gate, some cheeky lads, noting the housename and seeing Mrs. Melling, called out ... 'Look lads ... it's Pola Negri'. That lady was a famous silent screen star, probably forgotten today. Jess's mother, May, had a trick of turning on the glamour whenever she wished. She was very houseproud as most Lancashire women are. She would work dressed like a present-day bag-lady, then say ... 'Now for the transformation scene'. She would go upstairs, get washed and changed, and emerge looking as lovely as any film star. I remember her buying a 'Dolly Varden' hat, all trimmed with flowers. Her husband, Joe, said ... 'Our May could put a duster on her head and look bonny' ... and so she could. There's a little tribute to a lovely lady. To see her ready to go to a ball at the Guild Hall in the old Town Hall building, dressed in a spangled evening frock and smelling of Velouty Cream and Phul-Nana perfume was a delight to the senses and a joy to behold.

Childhood in Frenchwood is remembered as a golden age in spite of the signs of poverty and deprivation which still stalked the streets. Some houses had notices on their little gates reading 'No hawkers or circulars', for there were relicts from the war still peddling bootlaces and home-made soap, and little families still sang in the streets, the mothers carrying a tin mug for pennies. Some beggars were old soldiers who were without limbs, and dreadful to remember, sometimes the pathetic singers would start the dogs a-barking, I often shed tears for those poorer than us.

There were not many cars about; plenty of bikes, the ice-cream Eldorado man who had supplanted the ice-cream cart pulled by a pony, and the fishmonger with his swinging bucket at the back of the cart for the fish-heads. The local moggies, tails erect, would stalk the cart, and housewives with their plates handy would congregate where the fish-cart halted.

Yes, Frenchwood was special, unique almost, for there was a beautiful view of the Ribble from Frenchwood Knoll. We had the Strawberry Gardens, and Swillbrook, a steep winding runnelled lane leading down to Molly's Lane at the edge of Frenchwood Recreation Ground.

Bicyles had difficulty in negotiating this lane, for it was often awash. Bikes with worn tyres, rusting brake-blocks and rattling loose mudguards had problems. My bike was so ancient its back mudguard had little holes all along its edges where the strings had been to prevent long dressees from catching in the wheel-spokes. I was ashamed to be seen on it. The first thing I did when I earned my first wages was to buy a new Raleigh bicycle for four pounds ... paid for at two shillings and sixpence (or 2/6d) a week.

Lark Hill convent was a mystery place to us, although as kids from Grimshaw Street School we would try to see over the high wall which was topped with broken bottle-glass. We climbed on each other's shoulders to try to see the lake which we were told was in the grounds. We never did see it.

The little girls from the convent, all dressed in brown, would walk in crocodile formation with dignified gait down to Avenham Park in the company of stately gliding nuns.

Another crocodile, this time in grey sombre clothing and clattering polished clogs, would pass our house each day. They were the shorn-haired orphans from Shepherd Street Mission (in Oxford Street) on their way to school. They attended in 1928 the newly-opened Frenchwood Junior School. It had shiny new yellow coloured desks, with inkwells, so different from those at Grimshaw Street, where the old and cracked inkwells had black gunge at the bottom, therein the pen-nibs would become crossed so that a child would cry out ... 'Please, Miss, my nib's crossed', and then receive a new shiny pen-nib to replace the old one in its metal-tipped wooden penholder.

Mother always stood at her gate to smile and say hello to the children from the Mission; the older girls held the hands of the tinies, and the big boys in their oversized clogs brought up the rear of the crocodile.

A crocodile, a seasonal one, fascinated us children. We envied them, too, both for their dress and for what we imagined to be a life of excitement and glamour.

Frenchwood had many theatrical digs, and just off Oxford Street was a house which took in the little pantomime girls who appeared at Christmas time at the Preston Hippodrome. They had to attend school, and as they wended their way, a bright red crocodile, the girls in capes and shako-like hats with tassels on them, they were the envy of us kids in our sombre clothes. They had patent leather ankle-strap shoes and impressed us mightily. In the winter evenings, whilst we played around the gas-lamps with our orange-box ropes looped over the cross arm of the lamp to form a swing, shining our flash-lamps about in the darkness, we envied the girls who passed us by on their way to their evening's performance ... what a life!

Some of the semis, their owners fallen on difficult times in the thirties, took in such lodgers as G. H. Elliot, Reginald Dixon and other organists who played at the New Victoria Cinema, Preston. In the thirties one of the O'Donnell brothers lived close by, and reflected glory descended on us when North End won the cup in 1938.

I started this chapter recalling the sound of bells, the church bells, the convent bells, soon to be hushed and muffled because of the war. We could also hear the bell of the great Town Hall as it rang out for the hours and quarters and half-hours all over the roofs of Preston. We could see the clock well enough to tell the time from my Frenchwood home at the bottom end of Oxford Street. One day in March, 1947, when I had been married four years, I looked out to check the time, and there was no clock there. It was unbelievable, and I thought I must be dreaming. But, true enough, the clock tower and a lot of the building had gone ... and long gone is my Preston and Frenchwood childhood.

The last time I visited the area, all the streets were very quiet, not a child to be seen. Yet in my mind's eye paraded such a number of people, carts and horses, crocodiles of different hue, sad beggars, street traders of all sorts, housewives on their way to the corner shop or the Co-op, the nuns, the priests, the ice-cream sellers, the unemployed men who collected the 'snig-fry' from the Ribble at dead of night. The theatricals, the lads and lasses on their bikes, the little children with their baskets of Easter Eggs on their way to the park. The little orphans, the saucy dancers, the nuns and priests. And, saddest of all, the soldiers, sailors and airmen on their way to war.

The ones who did not come home to Frenchwood are not forgotten ... at least, not by me.

Lancaster Road, Preston

A Preston lady told me how she was 'browned up' to appear as an Indian lady in St. Matthew's procession of the Schools part in the 1922 Guild. She remembers that she wore a purple sari. Today, there would be no need to do this, for our lovely immigrant children could appear in their own colourful and beautifully decorative costumes.

This reminded me of the time in 1926 or thereabouts when I was instructed by mother not to stare at the sight of not one, but two coloured gentlemen walking along Lancaster Road, such an unusual sight to an eight-year-old. Or indeed to anyone then.

I had seen only one other dark-skinned man in Fishergate, previously ... 'A seaman', said Mother, 'from the docks', and I was told then not to stare at that phenomenon.

'Theatricals', snorted Mother with disapproval ... but she also 'tutted' as I gaped in wonderment at their companion.

Walking between them, elegantly dressed, and with a fur slung around her shoulders the size of a full-grown fox, was a lady who was a platignum blonde. That indeed was a rare sight in a Preston street of the twenties and, as she was without a hat, again a rare sight then. I saw that her hair was corrugated in deep marcel waves and she was made up, as Mother would have said ... 'to the nines'. Mothers did not hold with face powder and paint then, and big girls had to scrub their faces clean with spit on a hanky before going home! And as for wearing the new 'Tangee' lipstick, being advertised as 'kiss-proof' that really was encouraging devils' work to a Baptist parent.

The seaman I had gaped at had not had the romance, in my eyes, of the 'Theatricals' whom Father said later were the Artistes Layton and Johnson and their companion (I believe she was married to one of the pair), and they were probably appearing at one of our two Theatres in Tithebarn Street, not yet given over to the 'Talkies'. As a small girl, I was rather confused for, in Frenchwood, where I lived, in nearby Tiber Street, G. H. Elliott lodged at times. Mother had said he was the 'Chocolate Coloured Coon', but to my surprise, when he walked past my home, he was quite white — a hurrying sour-looking little fellow, in a long overcoat and black Homburg, whose lady companion walked slightly behind him, as though finding it difficult to match his springing steps.

Sixty years is a long time to keep such pictures in the mind, but for some reason Lancaster Road and nearby Crooked Lane remain with me to this day.

Lancaster Road held one or two excitements for me normally. There was a shop, a corn-chandlers called Lays, and in its window they often had lots of fluffy little chicks running about in the sawdust strewn window bottom.

Zinc water containers featured there, too, and the chicks, like tiny powder-puffs on skinny legs, were a delight to town-bred children who watched with their noses pressed to the glass.

Not such a pretty sight were the drunken men who always seemed to be rolling about from the several pubs along the way ... what a contrast to the innocent baby chickens. 'Don't stare', once again my Mother would say at the sight of the inebriated fellows! I was forever being told not to stare!

There was another shop which fascinated me as a child, close by the shop with the chickens. It was called Princes, and to me it was like an Aladdins cave, for it sold silverware, cut glass, lovely decorative lamps and great canteens of cutlery. My father frequently bought these lovely gifts, not for himself, but for the bowling prizes at Frenchwood Bowling Club at Avenham Park, where he was the secretary. The cutlery was in lovely oak boxes, lined with satin or velvet with a dozen of each of knives, forks and spoons of varying sizes. I can smell the French polish smell of those boxes now. There were servers, carvers, tiny teaspoons all shining and fascinating to a small girl. The shop sold Westminster chiming clocks, and the chimes, both tenor and baritone, striking the hours, and the halves and quarters rang out merrily. There were carriage clocks and clocks enclosed in glass, lovely vases of crystal, tea and dinner sets in China, statuettes and fruit sets in carnival glass. When it was time for the Fazackerley Shield to be competed for on the town's greens, the lovely shield was on display in the window. It was huge with a bas-relief of silver showing men bowling; there was a tree of raised silver in the background. It was a thing of great beauty. When it was presented on President's day, I often had the task of giving a bouquet to Mrs. Fazackerley. She was a tall lady and had to bend down to receive it. I tried to find out what happened to the lovely shield a few years ago, without luck.

Crooked Lane was just off Lancaster Road, there was a pub on the corner, then a few small cottages, two up and two down, the Ridings Corn Chandlers. My Grandma Livesey lived in the second one, rent three shillings and sixpence a week. When my cousin took it over at about 1926 she was cross because the landlord raised this to four shillings. The rooms were very small, the back kitchen flagged, and there was a cellar. The staircase was enclosed with a steep wooden staircase. There was an outside 'closet' which had a rectangular wooden seat and a green-painted door with a latch and bolt. Squares of newspaper hung from a string behind the door and there was always a smell of whitewash.

Sometimes the prickly chaff specks (which smelled like the inside of my Dad's straw boater) blew under the edge of the door and danced about one's dangling legs. As a child, I could only just clamber onto the high lavatory seat.

The living-kitchen of the cottage, with its iron fire-grate, high mantelshelf on which stood heroic iron horses with helmeted riders, had a brass bar underneath where clothes were hung, folded after they were ironed, to air. The clothes-rack was suspended from the ceiling of the back kitchen. There was always a bright fire, for Grandad was a coal merchant, his sister or aunt (I forget which) had a coal barge on the Preston to Lancaster canal. She was Great Aunt Ashworth. Often, in a rocking chair by the fire, sat Uncle Jack, who smoked a clay pipe and spat in the fire, so that the spittle hissed and crackled on the bars when his aim was poor. He never answered my questions. For instance, if I asked what the medals and trinkets displayed in a glass case were, he would tell me 'Lay o'ers to catch meddlers'. I found this very confusing, the word being so close to the word medals which I knew. Grandma, by contrast, was kind and loving. She never visited our house without bringing some small gift for me; it might be a penny lucky bag or some sherbert or a sugar mouse or a present wrapped up in thin coloured tissue-paper. She looked dignified in a sealskin cape, black jet-trimmed bonnet and long black clothes. But on one occasion at our house she lost her dignity and our cat suffered for it.

The cat, named 'Tush', had stolen some boiled ham from her carpet bag left hanging from the back of a chair. He got Grandma's little boot under his back-end and was propelled out of the back door like a rocket. He yowled in protest and his tail bushed out like a squirrel's and he was sworn at louder than his own feline cursing.

Because of the oft-told tale of the family history, I had, in my childish imaginings, almost endowed Grandma with royal forebears, but her behaviour on that occasion was anything but aristocratic, and certainly Uncle Jack (who spat) did not give the impression of having royal lineage! I was just a young pretender.

The story which so fired my fertile imagination is as follows:

My ancestor, Daniel Newby, was left as a baby on a doorstep in Kendal when the Scottish rebels passed through the town. It was in the year 1745, the fateful year of the Jacobite rebellion, and it was certainly fateful for Charles Edward Stuart, known as Bonnie Prince Charlie. The Highland soldiers passed by both in victory and, later, in defeat. Whether the foundling was abandoned on the march south or north I don't know. I used to picture the clansmen, kilted and draped in plaids pouring through the little town. They probably filled the townsfolk with fear so that they bolted their doors. So, whoever placed the little bundle on the step would not be seen. As a child, hearing the story, my imagination would take flight. How I wondered about the baby's parents. All little girls dream of being princesses or of having royal blood! Was the baby of royal descent? I was a great reader as a child, so I had plenty of stories to build upon. I had the pitiful picture in my mind of the child, wrapped in a torn plaid, soaked by the persistent rain, which history tells us bedevilled the Highlanders at Kendal. In my imaginings, the poor foundling would be crying pitifully for his faithless mother — I would almost cry myself at the thought of poor Daniel in the dark and cold of a winter's night. I never talked to my little friends of all this, not even to my Scots playmates, Elspeth and Mary. They came from Glasgow, and were fiercely proud of their heritage. If our little gang of children fell out, Mary would yell at us 'Yu English killed Mary Queen of Scots' and I would feel guilty about the sad royal lady ... I still do!

We all lived in Frenchwood at this time and our playground was not far from the River Ribble. Sometimes we would go on the Tram Bridge, which spans the river and from which can be seen the Southern bank and the fields to the South of Preston. I would look towards Walton-le-Dale, where the Prince's army camped, and picture the scene with its tents, wagons for the ammunition, and the horses. I did not tell the other children of my imaginings, in any case they were too interested in throwing stones into the whirlpools which lie close to the ancient bridge. My thoughts would linger again on the foundling who had his being (or so I believed) from one of that desperate army of Jacobites.

In the twenties, we were not force-fed with entertainment or potted histories on TV, as youngsters are today ... a lot of our entertainment was in the mind or, in truth, was self-made. My thoughts would run riot. I would ponder on the abandoned baby again ... what sort of person had placed him on the step in the hope of his being found? Was it a serving wench? Was it a lady's maid acting for her mistress? Was it a rough soldier depositing the child serving his master's orders ... could the master (fantastic thought) be the one who was the Young Pretender? I was the one who had the pretensions.

Father said that young Daniel was probably the child of a camp follower. I remember asking 'What's a camp follower?'

Nobody told me, and even my big brother didn't know the answer ... I knew he went to Cunningham's Camp at the Isle of Man. I went to Brownie camp, too, but didn't know anything of followers. On a nostalgic trip to my home town last year, I again visited Lancaster Road and Crooked Lane.

There's still a pub on the corner, but just along the lane is a small park-like area with young saplings, greenery and a few seats. It's just where the tiny cottages and the corn-chandlers used to stand. Dozens of waddling pigeons, fat-rumped, short-legged, like overfed middle-aged women pottering along to market, were foraging, self-importantly and bossily, in the sunlight as I paused. They seemed to be in a quarrelsome mood, at odds with the beauty of the May morning.

I wondered, whimsically, if these birds of the nineties, were descendents of the many who had harassed my four-year-old self when I had played in the backyard of Number 2 Crooked Lane so long ago.

Now, as a seventy-year-old, I pondered ... did some atavistic sense bring these present-day pigeons back there where there had once been a corn merchants on the very same spot? In the past it must have been a birds' paradise. Had they now, literally, come home to roost and feed, where once, to my certain knowledge, Ridings Corn Merchants had traded, and were these strutting birds visiting by instinct the land of their fathers?

There I stood, lonely now, on this quiet Sabbath, where my own roots were (on the land of my mothers) so transfixed by the past I almost felt rooted to the spot. I was glad that there was no-one about to see the gathering tears.

I stepped from the pavement, the well-worn pavement, on to the grass, just where the remembered vestibule with its blue and white tiles had been. There had been a polished brass strip, too, and the little inner door had had starred opaque glass in it. I saw in my memory's eye the high mantelshelf with the horses, the glass cabinet, the fire-range and oven. I felt the presence of Grandma Livesey and Uncle Jack. He was bearded and frightening, she apple-cheeked, sloe-black eyes, and black garbed.

As I closed my eyes, remembering, I could 'hear' the chandler's cart, horse-drawn, rumbling down the cobbled lane of long ago. It used to be high-stacked with sacks and bales and the air smelled of grain or hay.

If the cart had to pause outside the net-curtained small-paned window, the whole little room was darkened. I would then be allowed to give the whiskery-muzzled horse a crust. Often the sloping lane was awash with strong-smelling urine as it frothed along down to Lancaster Road.

It was an effort to pull myself back to the present, and I had to collect my solitary self to face the day. My last thought then was for my own mother, who had lived just there. I pictured her in her later life, plump as a pigeon herself then, and I almost felt her hold out her hand and heard her say ... 'Time to go now, Kathie', as she had said so many times when I had stood in this same spot more than sixty years ago. Time, indeed, to go, to step back into the present in this Preston street, and to leave the family ghosts to themselves.

I shook myself in the early morning chill, the sun had not yet warmed the air ... Time to come back to the lonely present, time to forget the 'Young Pretender' of my childish imaginings. Time, too, for me to stop being an old pretender. I sat down on one of the benches which was just about where my three-legged stool had stood so long ago. I thought about the present and my many grandchildren, and that I would tell them the tale of Daniel Newby, foundling of 1745, who lives on somewhere in his many descendants, and his name is not forgotten.

Our Gracie

Many years ago, when I gave a talk on Woman's Hour, the producer said to me 'We didn't quite know what to expect, you coming from Rochdale.' I think she expected to see a woman wearing clogs and shawl and speaking with an 'Eeh Bah Gum' accent. I felt I was a disappointment to her when she said ... 'Come along now ... where's that lovely Lancashire accent?' Her name was Isobel and I remember her well. I'd never been to London before, and certainly never broadcast, so was a little awe-struck to respond as I should have done. Still, it was all a great experience. Jean Metcalfe was the presenter of the programme, a lady guaranteed to put anyone at ease, so it was really great fun.

Normally, when one mentions Rochdale to folk in other parts of England, or even abroad, Gracie's name crops up and questions are usually asked about her. (Though I do recall one time, on the Isle of Capri, an Italian boy didn't know about Rochdale, so I said it was near to Manchester ... that made his bright eyes sparkle ... 'Ah, Signora ... Manchester UNITED', he cried, booting an empty shoe box across the carpet of the elegant shoe-shop where I was buying sandals. He narrowly missed a stately Italian lady who was carrying a French poodle and who skipped out of the way of the shoe-box with the grace of a Georgie Best). You don't get such exuberance in Saxone's, do you? The mention of Rochdale to some elicits the fact that the town is known for being the birth-place of the Co-operative movement, and it's surprising how many Canadians or Australians, and even Chinese people, know of the Co-op connection.

When I told people I worked in the same street as the one in which Gracie Fields was born, they always asked about it and whether I could tell them of the little chip shop which was still standing in the fifties and early sixties. Then Number Nine still had the plaque on its crumbling walls which announced that ... Grace Stansfield, known as Miss Gracie Fields, Freeman of this Borough, was born at 9 Molesworth Street on 9th January, 1898. The shop, before it was demolished, was a sorry sight. It was flanked by squalid shops once patronised by the workers from the nearby mills, workshops and the brewery. The only brightness in the ready-for-demolition area came from the brilliant rainbow-coloured clothes of the ever-increasing immigrant population. Front doors were painted in yellows and purples, or even two-toned. Front steps were not donkey-stoned as in the old days, and on one cold and windy Monday morning when I was observing this, a mangy dog was lifting its leg above a cardboard container of milk. Door jambs were certainly not carefully scrubbed and stoned as in the days when proud Lancashire housewives made such a chore their weekly commitment.

Friday night was always step-cleaning and window-cleaning times in the old days when Gracie was a lass. I contemplated at the time I passed on this grey morning the dark and dirty window of the little shop, noting that it was still showing grimy adverts for cigarettes and thinking that its tinny shop-bell would never ring again to admit a customer. Nearby, a tree festooned with dirty paper and with empty bottles nestling by its straggling roots added to the desolation of the street.

And yet ... there was a little plot of land further along, wire netted about, in which, reaching hopefully up towards the light, hundreds of tiny buds, green and sweet, thrusting forth from their dispirited and aged parent-bush, were striving for survival in the workaday Rochdale soil, half a world away from Capri and Gracie's home of that time.

How strange and splendid to think that, in the bedroom above the shop in Molesworth Street, blossomed forth (just like the buds) the girl, Grace Stansfield, with the voice that could bring forth tears as well as laughter. How she herself would have laughed if she had heard what one Rochdale housewife said on a bus going to Littleborough one day. It was just prior to Gracie's visit to the town to receive the Freedom of the Borough. The woman was heard to complain bitterly ... because the lions on the Town Hall balcony had been given a coat of expensive paint ... 'Just because Gracie's coming here, they've even GELDED t'lions at front o't'Town 'All.' (I remember there were similar complaints of extravagance when the Queen visited us and a new lavatory was installed in the Town Hall ... there were even more complaints when it was discovered that Her Majesty didn't even use it!). No Royal Flush, so to speak!

My favourite memory of Gracie Fields is seeing her at a Command Performance which was shown on television. She had just had the huge audience laughing uproariously at one of her comic songs; it could have been 'The Biggest Aspidistra in the World' or maybe 'Walter, Walter, take me to the Altar', and the applause was going on and on. To silence this, she turned with her back to everyone, then, as quietness came, she slowly turned, and the orchestra stuck up for the song 'Three Green Bonnets'. It's a song about three little girls, Dulcie and Daisy and Dorothy May. It ends with them being old ladies, and the three bonnets 'grown old unawares, hanging on three pegs at the foot of the stairs...'. Then the last lines tell that 'Blue eyes are swollen, and so are the grey ... for the angels have taken Dear Dorothy May.' The song, sung quietly, and yet every word clear as a bell, enraptured the audience. There was this deafening silence then, which we know means that deep emotion is almost too much to be acknowledged, or else that there are thoughts that 'do lie too deep for tears'. WHAT an ARTISTE was 'Our Gracie.'

The plaque is now set in stonework in a minute patch of greenery close by where the little chip shop once stood. It is well-tended, which is good, for the people who once had the pleasure of seeing Gracie Fields perform are rapidly diminishing. We do, of course, have the Gracie Fields Theatre in Rochdale, and maybe her singing shade adds its musical accompaniment when young Rochdalians perform for our pleasure. But we, being mortal, have not the ears to hear her.

The Brewery

Molesworth Street, Rochdale, which was named after a former Vicar of St. Chad's, which is the Parish Church, besides being the street where Gracie Fields was born at No. 9, was also where the town's brewery stood until 1970. Now only the building which was the boiler-house still stands, for it was a late addition to what had originally been Rochdale & Manor Brewery and which was later owned by Samual Smith of Tadcaster.

In 1961, when I went to work there in the office, it was like stepping back into a former age, for it was a place of Dickensian high desks, coal fires, polished linoleum-covered floors, and whose telephone switchboard was like something from a museum. My typewriter was of the sit-up-and-beg variety, and the windows fronting the street were of engraved glass showing the brewery's old name. A workman from the boiler-house would stoke up our office fire each morning, and fill up our coal-scuttle for the day. There were no such things as calculators — everything was added up in one's head, even the wages cards, and should a workman think his wage was wrong, he had to come to a little window which was raised to hear his bitter complaint. At the same window, mothers would arrive towing reluctant lads whose necks would be covered in erupting boils. The mothers would be requesting some brewery yeast with which to dose their spotty offspring, for it was believed that the frothy, creamy and very smelly stuff would make the skin of the embarrassed boy as smooth as that of a baby! If we office staff felt in need of a tonic, we, too, would revive ourselves with a large spoonful of the yeast ... it worked wonders! At the same window at Christmas time, members of the public could actually purchase wines and spirits, for the brewery held a licence and the name of the secretary of the Brewery was over the door of No. 86, just as if it were a pub.

Not many people knew this, and we were pleased about it, but we certainly were kept busy in the festive season, receiving payment for beers, wines and spirits.

Because I felt my family would benefit from yeast, I often took a jar-full home and one day on the bus I was carrying a particularly lively jar of it. I sat behind a little man who was in the seat behind the driver. He fell asleep, head on his chest, for there was an air about him of having drunk well if not wisely. In those days there was a dark blind behind the driver's partition, and just before setting off he raised it with a great clatter and, as it shot up, the cheerful imbiber leapt to his feet crying ... 'Eeh ... it's dayleet', then promptly subsided again. Just then my yeast erupted, pushing off its loose lid, and cascaded all down the front of my pale blue coat with a very pungent beery aroma. Everyone looked at the little chap with disgust and blamed him for reeking of beer! I quietly covered my yeast with my scarf and held my nose high.

To work at a brewery somehow made one cheerful, for there was a cheerfulness about the men, probably due to their allowance, a very popular 'perk' indeed. It was nice to type letters about 'Kent Fuggles' and 'Worcester Goldings', those lovely names for the hops used in brewing. On brewing days, the air was warm with the heady smell which floated over the town, and farmers called, some with horse-drawn carts, to collect the beery-smelling grain for cattle feed. On such times I would recall being a schoolgirl in Preston where my elementary school was in the same street as two little beer-houses which brewed their own. The landlords would throw the spent grain out onto the pavement for collection and the steaming pile was just right for jumping over and falling into before we were sent packing.

The allowance for the men was two pints a day, officially, but if a fellow happened to be a non-drinker, his pal would do very nicely, thank you ... all the men were allowed the same; the tradesmen, such as coopers or painters or joiners, got the same ... plus whatever they could scrounge ... often a fellow might be well over the odds, but very few workers had cars then, more likely a bicycle! It was quite a common sight to see a painter with brush in one hand and a pint pot in the other as he worked. Sometimes caution was thrown to the winds, perhaps because of the chance to enjoy the 'allowance', and one time when it was time to go home, the painter could not be found. In time, he was discovered fast asleep on the roof of one of the buildings and made a shaky descent on the ladder which had given his presence away. Another time, the joiner did a complicated side-step along a newly-attached

War-time shopping at the Co-op (Your Caring Sharing Co-op)

"A reet good job" at the Manchester & Salford Co-op (Your Caring Sharing Co-op)

Searching for a victim of the 1930s' depression in the River Ribble (Frenchwood, Preston)

A clogger's shop (Your Caring Sharing Co-op)

"Our Gracie" taking tea with the Mayor and Mayoress (Our Gracie)

A SECOND HELPING

The Park School, Winckley Square (Memories of a Winckle)

Preston Whit Walks — 1920s (A Preston Whit Monday)

A flat cap and a load of bull (1922 Guild Memories)

Where the moulds were made for Margerison's Soap Works Preston Guild exhibits (Photograph c.1880) (The White Windsor Soap Works, Preston)

Preston Station Free Buffet in war-time. That could be me with the jug! (Sixty Years On)

Ice skating in Avenham Park, Preston, in the '30s (Sixty Years On)

Sold at Co-operative Stores Only.

C.W.S. CORSETS

COMBINE

EASE AND FIT.

HERE ARE THREE SPECIAL BARGAINS.

Made at the C.W.S. Works — at — Desborough.

5s. 6d.
The Marvel.
Dove Colour.

6s. 6d.
GB 211a.
Dove and White.

7s. 6d.   The Ellesmere
Dove Colour.

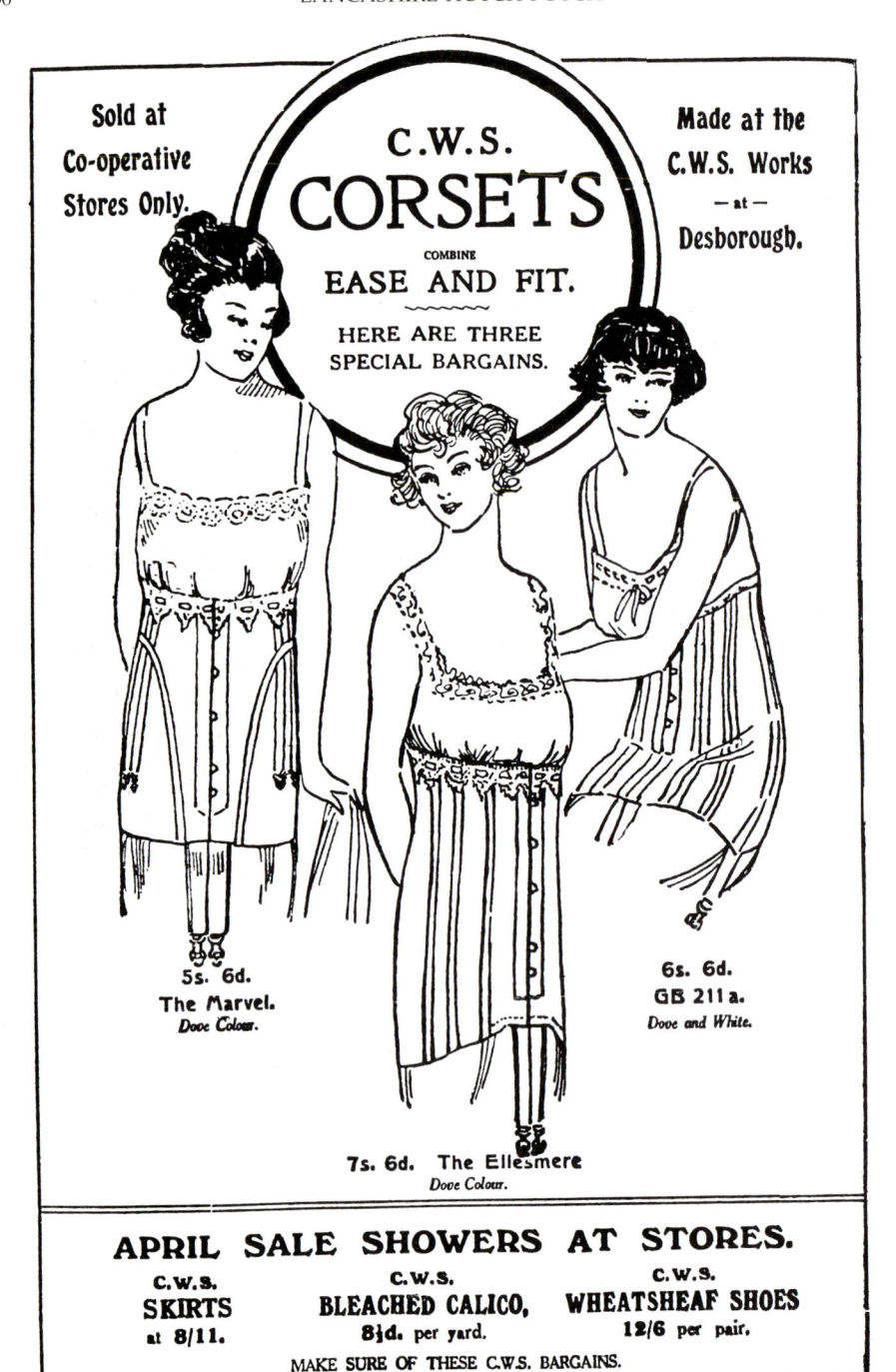

APRIL SALE SHOWERS AT STORES.

| C.W.S. SKIRTS at 8/11. | C.W.S. BLEACHED CALICO, 8½d. per yard. | C.W.S. WHEATSHEAF SHOES 12/6 per pair. |

MAKE SURE OF THESE C.W.S. BARGAINS.

In their full and fascinating flesh (Monkey Runs)

Eeh oop lads (Monkey Runs)

guttering, much to everyone's concern ... 'Me name's Bird, I can fly', he announced cheerfully — fortunately he didn't put it to the test! He told us stories of when he was a young sailor wearing a broad-brimmed straw sailor-hat and how he came home once on shore-leave to Rochdale and had to walk along the 'Landing' in Rochdale's Oldham Road. He remembers his hat with its broad band sailing off his head in a high wind and floating along on the nearby canal.

He would scare the office girls when he climbed high ladders if working indoors, for he looked so unsteady, he would repeat that he could fly, and one day flew off the top step and landed on the office floor. 'I'll be alreet when I've collected me Oil', he chirruped, meaning his allowance. Yes, they were barmy as well as balmy days in the brewery at Molesworth Street. Occasionally there was trouble and recrimination when the wrong 'plug' was pulled out or else not replaced after the cleaning of a great steel vessel, and dozens of gallons of beer would flood out down into the River Roche, perhaps to the delight of the rampaging river rats who maybe thought that their birthdays had come!

One of our older workers told lovely tales. He had only four fingers on one hand and he would threaten playfully to give anybody a 'bunch of fours'. He told stories of how our Rochdale men would travel to Tadcaster for a brewery cricket match. The Yorkshiremen would be in cricket 'whites', but only our Head Brewer owned such wear. Our chaps had wide grey flannels, or dark trousers of serge, and only gym shoes or even cracked boots. Having drunk heartily on the way, the cabbage fields of Tadcaster were well watered during the match and the sturdy Yorkshiremen frowned upon their brothers from across the border.

Many tales were told of the kindness of our workmen. At Christmas they collected old toys from the tip and painted and repaired them for needy children. Old strappings of leather were used to sole shoes for folks who had little money. There was the tale of the 'fire-beater', so called even when in my time the boilers were changed to 'oil-fired' — who once took a supply of coal and dropped it down the cellar-hole of a needy woman's house in Livesey Street. Unfortunately, the gift was dropped into the wrong cellar, and the surprised recipient looked upon his windfall, or should it be coal-fall, as a gift from the gods. There is just a patch of grass where once the office of the brewery stood, and other industrial units have taken the place of the old brewery, gone, like Gracie's birth-place, for ever, except in the minds of an ever-dwindling number of Rochdalians.

Doin' Me Front

You would have to be a Prestonian or a Rochdalian, for example, to have heard that, and you would need to be of a certain age, too. For the days are long gone when Friday evening of every week was set aside for the ritual of donkey-stoning the front steps and window-sills of each terrace home.

Surrounds or door-jambs of each front door had to be washed or stoned, too, for dirty dogs had a bad habit of cocking a leg there if a lamp-post were not convenient. Some housewives, dressed in 'pinnies' made out of sacking, even swilled and mopped down the flags in front of their domains, and any woman not fond of such chores was called 'A dirty Bet', or perhaps it was hinted that 'she was no better than she should be!' Any woman with dirty lace curtains was especially frowned upon. Back yards were swilled down and scrubbed with great bristly brushes and husbands cleaned the upstairs windows by sitting on the sill, backside protruding over the street, legs anchored by the sashed window, and then they plied the 'shammy leather' to good effect. Our family, Lancashire folk though we were, had, by much scrimping and saving, progressed to a semi-detached in the twenties, so my mother did not have to bother too much to keep her 'front' in the good order which neighbours of terrace homes expected. It was not until I encountered a typical Lancashire housewife that I realised that I had many short-comings in her eyes ... I felt very inadequate then ...

It was in the early forties. My husband was what was called in those days, when Army Officers often rose from the ranks, 'A Temporary Gentleman'. Truth to tell, he was far prouder of having been a Grenadier Guardsman than being an officer, for to be a Guardsman who had endured the punishing training was proof positive that he was a MAN!

I suppose, as his wife, I may have been considered a 'temporary lady' and my husband was billeted (and I with him) in rooms in Wales. The landlady was an Oldhamer and thus I learned what might be expected when, after the War, I would live in Oldham. I had a foretaste of what was to come when I might have my own home away from Preston.

Although the lady was kind to me, realising I was a newly-wed, she read me frequent lectures on how all her furniture was treated with bees-wax, and that I must be sure to use mats under every cup and saucer, she expected me to polish everything in sight once a week, and she informed me that she was so particular that the very bed-springs were oiled with oil-of-lavender. (I wondered if she was trying to tell me something, but I was too shy to ask!). My husband had a batman (where was Robin, my grandchildren ask) who laid the fire for us. Our landlady must have counted the coals, for she often complained that, unlike the colliers who lives in the village, SHE did not get a coal allowance. I spent my days feeling guilty, for I fell so far short of her principles of good housewifery. She even informed me that she and her husband NEVER shared the bathroom, when I was only brushing my teeth as my husband shaved. 'I've never undressed without first putting the light out,' she informed me, and I wondered if all Lancashire ladies were so bashful. Things must surely have changed in nearly fifty years!

My first home after I left Preston was such a happy little house, and I firmly believe that houses retain something of their owners. This one had large lighter patches on the wallpaper where framed family pictures of grandparents had been, and there were picture-rails and a clothes-rack in the living room.

Of course, there were no fitted units, but the houseproud elderly lady who came before me had hung a curtain below the yellow slop-stone in the tiny back kitchen. This was a common practice as it hid the space between the brick pillars which supported the sink and where the Chloros, bucket, scrubbing brushes and donkey-stones were kept. A tiny table, three-legged stool and brown-painted cupboard and a grey and white mottled gas cooker filled up the rest of the space. No wonder we elderly folk envy the young-married of today who have all 'mod-cons' in their dream kitchens.

What we did have in plenty in our little house were mice. The little blighters left tiny paw-prints in the solidified fat of my chip pan if I left it uncovered.

I think they must have skated about on my hall linoleum, for it was very highly polished. Trying to keep up with the standard of the local women encouraged me to shine the linoleum each week, too. Unfortunately, when I had occasion to call in a plumber, he stood on my doormat behind the front door and shot clean down the hallway like a bullet, landing up at the bottom of the narrow staircase. He said I should have had 'Warning' on my mat and not 'Welcome'. I decided to save up for a strip of carpet. Very few little homes had fitted carpets then, in fact we had so little compared to today in our houses.

When we moved to a bigger house at the top of the 'brew', I learned about Cardinal Polish, for the Accrington brick gardens walls; and the coping stones on them, in some cases, were actually polished with the red greasy stuff. I could hardly believe my eyes! Kitchen floors were shined with it also, and back steps and back window-sills. Front ones were donkey-stoned, excepting some which were painted cream ... they had to be washed each week, usually on the same day. Some of the old brigade of housewives thought that was cheating. One neighbour told me that some women would have polished the tram-lines, too, if they hadn't risked being mowed down by the tram! I felt very inadequate in my house, with its pointed gable and leaded windows ... it was considered 'posh' to have your windows leaded. (At least we didn't get bothered by double-glazing and window-replacement salesmen then). Perhaps the windows were made to fit better in those days. Also, the spending of such large sums to tradesmen would have been considered a luxury then, though it's taken for granted now.

What would have been thought of as an 'Ideal Home' and beyond our means as being only for the well-to-do are considered to be the just reward for folk who work hard and perhaps, too, for those who don't.

Nowadays, every housewife aspires to a 'Dream Kitchen'. Salespeople harass us with advertising, even with phone calls, to let them plan for us a kitchen of our dreams. Exhibitions of gigantic size tempt the houseproud to spend thousands of pounds on kitchens fit for a queen.

Such displays of our times remind me of a long-ago trades fair of the twenties. My friend Nellie made an exhibition of herself — and her blushing mother and father — when she saw not only a latter-day dream kitchen, but a nightmare kitchen as well. In the twenties, trade exhibitions were on quite a small scale. In Preston, the Public Hall was the venue for such events in the autumn. Hygiene was being brought to the attention of the people and, to such ends, I remember two side-by-side mock-up kitchens on display, to encourage attention to clean living of a practical kind.

I can still clearly see the 'Right Kitchen', where milk jugs were covered with little lace nets, a-dangle with shiny blue beads. The firegrate and side oven were black-leaded to a satin-like finish. The large fireguard, colourful rag-rug and bright brass fender with its fire-irons were proof of the presence of a diligent houseproud woman. Windows gleamed, food was covered, pans shone. Crockery was neatly stacked on shelves edged with lacy shelf paper. Matches were out of reach of small hands and a contented stuffed cat slept in its special basket. The table, covered with a snowy white cloth, was laid for tea with cups and saucers, and a big brown tea pot on a stand was placed well away from the edge of the table. Wax spills stood in a jar on the high mantelshelf and heroic, helmeted, black-iron riders on excited, rearing horses looked slightly out of place at each end of it. Little notices abounded giving advice to those too slow to take in the visual messages of clean living. An extra-large notice read: 'Is This Like Your Kitchen?' In direct contrast was the 'Nightmare Kitchen'. Fly-papers, thick with bluebottles, hung from the bracket of the gas light. Tatty clothes were festooned from the lop-sided clothes-rack. There was no fireguard, milk was uncovered, and an inquisitive cat explored the uncovered food on the table. A stuffed mouse or two eyed a lump of cheese on the table. Worse, the cloth hung well over the edge, beneath which a waxen model of a child was giving it a tug, so that the teapot was in danger of descending upon its not-too-clean head. 'It This Like Your Kitchen?' asked the notice. Poor Nellie, studying both as she held her parents' hands, squeaked loudly: 'Ours is like that', as she pointed to the shabby one. She had, as they say, opened her mouth and put her little clog in it. She was whisked away by her loving, if feckless, mum so that her little clog-irons sparked across the floor of the Public Hall — when her feet touched, that is.

I was there, too, on that long-gone evening, thrilled to be given a balloon with 'Liptons Tea' printed on it and a tiny paper-thin celluloid fish which curled up in the palm of a warm hand ... like magic. Like magic, too, an 'Oriental' gentleman (probably an unemployed cotton worker dressed as a Chinaman) sold little 'shells' which blossomed into flowers when placed into water. What simple delights for a twenties child. There were stalls selling curling-tongs for producing Marcel waves in hair, and Morgans' Pomade to be rubbed on bald pates. My dad bought some of this and mother was not pleased, for he had lately taken to worrying about his baldness. Mother thought he had his eye on a lady whom we children disliked, for she used 'Evening in Paris' scent, strong enough to make the eyes water. She also used white face-powder which nestled in her wrinkles and she dyed her hair (little children then, as now, don't miss much). I associate the exhibition with mother's interest in having a blue rinse on her hair and her worry about her looks for she, totally unused to make-up, lingered at a stall where a demonstrator mixed together face-powder of varying hues. Our mother bought some; that was so unusual that it filled us with dread. Surely it was not right, surely our dad, who was quite old (at least in his forties by our reckoning) was not about to stray? Mother purchasing face-powder was cause for concern. There were dark murmurings amongst the children of our family. All the pomade did was stain the pillows yellow and dad remained as bald as a melon, except for his outcrop of gingery hair. Mother looked alien to us with powder on her face and we children complained and soon things were back to normal. Fancy ideas from exhibitions were not for us, though we delighted in the Palm Court orchestra and the magic lantern show. We saw an electric vacuum cleaner for the first time at the Public Hall and we gathered round to watch the salesman demonstrate how cake-crumbs leaped about in the draught as they were sucked into the cleaner; that was magical, too. Mother cleaned her one carpet with a stiff brush, tea-leaves and bran and it was many a long day before every household had a vacuum cleaner.

Trade exibitions then, as now, showed luxuries to tempt buyers to spend too much money. But in the twenties we were not offered, as today, endless credit to purchase dream kitchens which may — if money becomes even scarcer — turn into nightmare kitchens. I wonder if little Nellie ever got a kitchen different from the nightmare one of 60 years ago?

Memories of a Winckle

As a new girl at the Junior Park School, Winckley Square, Preston, sixty-one years ago, it was the smell of Ronuk polish which was the first impression, remembered to this day.

Secondly, as we entered the oak-beamed panelled hall, with its blue-velvet curtained stage, with white proscenium arch, was that we eleven-year-olds, some fee-paying, some scholarship girls, were asked to sit, cross-legged, on the gleaming polished parquet floor.

To some of us, fresh from Elementary Schools, such as Grimshaw Street, which had board floors full of splinters, or flagged floors, and where we sat on forms which, though well polished by rough-trousered backsides, or flannel-bloomered bottoms, could still inflict occasional scars from nails or 'spells', this was a novelty.

Nervously, on this our first day at a new school, we glanced up to the high ceiling, where thick climbing ropes were looped up out of the way, and wondered fearfully if we would be expected to shin up them to reach the very beams.

Then there were the pictures... the copies by great artists which adorned the walls, for we had time to study them as the assembly increased in size as more and more little girls filed in.

Some looked apprehensive, some cheerful, but all had one thing in common. This was the uniform, strictly enforced. Navy blue gymslips with velvet yoke, white blouses with silver and navy blue striped tie and long black stockings. All would be wearing navy blue knickers, and some of us fleecy-lined Liberty bodices, with rubber buttons to which suspenders were attached. The gymslips had to be long enough to touch the calves when kneeling, and on the first gym lesson (Miss Francis, who wore her hair in ear-phone style, with tape-measure in hand, made sure of this).

I was at the end of a row, near the back, and so had a close view of the nearby copies of the oil-paintings.

There was one of Miss Bowles, by Reynolds. She was a simpering miss, all frills and furbelows, and she had her pet dog in quite a stranglehold with her chubby childish arms. Quite appropriate in an all-girls school.

Cheek-by-jowl with her with Frans Hals' 'Laughing Cavalier'. How worldly-wise, impudent and salacious was the gentleman with his elaborate lace collar, wide black hat and cheeky grin. I used to think that he should not be eyeing us, when, later in that first term, we were upended on the ropes with our bloomers in full view!

Perhaps other old girls who attended the school from 1907 onwards (and one of them wrote to me a couple of years ago, saying she was one of the cornerstones of the school) could ever forget the aura of gentility we encountered in the old world charm of this great house which had originally been the home of the Miller family of Preston. First it had been called Preston High School and was intended for the daughters of gentlemen. Only later were scholarship girls allowed in. That was a thrill to those of us who had been to schools where only religious pictures and maps adorned our darkly-painted walls. There, Jesus fed the five thousand, or presided over the Last Supper, and the maps had shiny red patches ... 'Our Empire'. We girls of slender means were now introduced, by way of the old masters ... to a little bit of culture!

Not that we were devoid of a little culture in my home, for we had 'Between Two Fires' and 'The Boyhood of Raleigh' hanging from our picture rail in our living room. The pictures had been obtained by coupons from packets of Gold Flake cigarettes (11½d for twenty) and I was mightily impressed as I studied the faraway look in Master Raleigh's eyes — he would have been more suitable than the Laughing Cavalier, I felt sure, to grace the school's walls.

'Winckles' of my age who attended the school in the late twenties, and who were from elementary schools, must have been a little awed by the building itself, with its main sweeping staircase and the little oak staircase with minstrel gallery which led to the upper third forms. Marble fireplaces, parquet floors and oak panelling were in strange contrast to the rough-floored and green and brown painted walls of old and bare council schools. But now we had entered another world and mixed with pupils many of whom took luxuries for granted. How shy, yet proud, we felt to be part of this new environment. Today's children would rightly know that all should expect only the best for their education ... but also that they should value it, we hope.

In our new school classrooms we had coal fires, adding such a cosy air. There was always a scuttle-full of coals, and we had a 'fire monitor' to do the stoking, using a black velvet mitten placed handily by; actually, it hung from the knob of the bell-pull which had once been used to summon servants from way down below. We also had a door-monitor, whose job it was to see that girls marched quietly in single file. She also had to close the door after a mistress had entered and we had all stood to attention. In the upper school later, such a monitor, prefect or teacher stood by the outer cloakroom door to inspect our faces for any trace of powder ... the idea of lipstick on a schoolgirl was too horrendous to be contemplated then!

All girls had to change into 'ward-shoes', strapped, flat-heeled, round-toed, on entering school. Gym shoes had to have their special draw-stringed bag, often made from a discarded shirt-lap (just the right size for doubling over into a bag). Hockey boots had their own spaces under a long form under the hook-racks in the flagged cloakroom. I remember that I hated my boots because they were really boys' boots, heavily studded by my dad, and therefore cheaper than the real thing. Being ever so slightly different was anathema then to a child, just as it is now.

In summer we wore Panama hats, and in the winter velour brimmed ones. It was considered 'posh' to have one in 'peach-velour'. This type had a fluffier finish than the commoner sort. Both winter and summer hats had the silver and navy hat band with Preston's Lamb and Flag insignia at the front. Whichever sort of Panama was worn, be it cheap or expensive, if rained upon it always rose up in the centre like a bun with too much baking-powder in it! To have taken off the hat and gone bare-headed, or to wear it at an angle, was unthinkable.

One mistress was particularly incensed if a girl fell from the high standards set as regards being correctly dressed and ladylike. She made sure our hands were gloved as we left school. She stuck to the precept regarding the Junior School pupils that 'it was beneficial that they were taught the rules and customs of the school before merging into larger numbers of the upper school at Moor Park'. To loll against a lamp-post at a tram-stop, or to eat sweets in the street, was a 'crime' then to us, and I still would avoid such a transgression today, so well was the need for dignified behaviour preached then.

All the teachers were unmarried then, or possibly widowed, for it was only later that married women were allowed to teach (when it became expedient). There was only one mistress whom I recall with less than delight. She it was who asked all scholarship girls to hold up their hands on the first day at the big school. We were then lectured on our special need to work hard and thus repay the townsfolk of Preston to whom we owed thanks for our education!

Of course, we should have been proud of our status, but young girls do not always have their values organised at such a time ... I only know I felt humiliated, for which I am now ashamed. On another occasion, with the same lady, I vividly recall that when a girl called Dorothy Richmond, a girl with vivid red hair, was caught wearing perfume, she was lectured and told the tale of Henry the Eighth, who carried a pomander to disguise his unpleasant body odour. Poor Dorothy blushed to match her glorious hair.

The ninety-year-old, who wrote to me three years ago and said she was practically a cornerstone of the Junior Park School, still remembers it with pleasure. As so indeed do I, and particularly the lovely mistresses who taught at the school.

Miss O'Dell, a darkly pretty Irish teacher who taught chemistry, on instructing me to carry out an experiment at home, told me to 'Ask Cook for some flour when you get home'. I did not tell her we had no such luxury in our house as I secretly pictured my plump little mother knocking hell out of a great lump of dough in her big brown and yellow bread-baking bowl. Girls were girls to Miss O'Dell. To us she was adorable and many other teachers are remembered, too, with great affection.

Dear Miss Booth, the senior gym mistress, with her neat shingled hair, was so slim that the pleats of her gymslip were always deep and flat, whereas some plump little girls had gymslips whose pleats spread out like the staves of a bursting barrel.

Miss Booth's leather gym shoes always shone, her seamed woollen stockings were always taut on shapely legs, they did not concertina down on skinny shanks as some of ours did. There was one schoolgirlish sin which earned her wrath, and an order mark (three such marks and you were before the Headmistress). Our stocking-tops had to meet up with our elasticated knicker-legs, there had to be NO GAP.

If that occurred, and a strip of flesh be on view at any time in the lesson, we were awarded an order mark for having what was termed a 'smile' ... that exposure of white flesh, and in consequence a suspender, too. No sergeant major in the Brigade of Guards was stricter than dear Miss Booth when it came to appearances! She taught us to cry 'Hip hip huRRAH' rather than 'HooRAY' when raising our hockey sticks in salute to a winning opposing team. Some of us had to learn to iron out our Lancashire vowels, too, and say 'How Now Brown Cow' in elocution lessons!

Miss Duxbury, who taught French, always wore such pretty, colourful clothes, quite unusual then in a teacher. She would make the lessons interesting by telling us of her holidays in France with her sister.

Some of the Staff had double-barrelled names which I fear we shortened privately. It will take an old girl like myself to know who 'Miss HumpyTed' and 'Miss BlackyBee' were. We were delighted because the former used to keep her handkerchief in her knicker leg, just as we did, for the pockets on our bloomers were always too small!

A booklet written by Miss Alice M. Stoneman, the first headmistress, mentions that the school opened in October, 1907, but it was formally opened on January 16th, 1908. On January 19th, one of the two others days dedicated to the opening when all and sundry could attend, it was a Saturday and there was a match at Preston North End, and many visitors arrived at school after the match. (This, of course, was at Moor Park, for the Junior Park School in Winckley Square was not used till 1918, being taken over from what had been Preston High School for Girls). However, at Moor Park on the visitors' day mentioned, several mistresses had to decline invitations to tea from visitors, and also had to refuse tips! It was noted that groups of all sorts of people attending behaved with courtesy and order throughout!

In the same little book, Miss Stoneman relates that in the 1914 war girls from the school collected sphagnum moss from Longridge, which was used for medicinal purposes for war-wounded soldiers.

As I said, all women teachers were unmarried in those days, and many were gentle ladylike souls whom we girls loved. Some were too gentle and, I'm ashamed to say, we sometimes took advantage of this. There were others, of course, who strode about manfully in their polished brogues ... we kept our eyes down and trod carefully with them, but they were really very fair with us and perhaps realised how unsure we were.

We only had one male teacher (of music), Doctor Lofthouse, and Miss Cooper chaperoned us then, marking exercise books on the pretty little blue-velvet curtained stage as we piped through 'Linden Lee' and 'The Skye Boat Song'.

Miss Cooper, always dressed in brown with little cream collars to her frocks, was a firm favourite. She was so motherly and kind to us girls, and should we even begin to misbehave in the singing class, a reproving look over her glasses was enough to silence us.

We had one teacher who is especially remembered for being totally human and down to earth. She was Miss Mildred Whiteing. She did not have a string of letters after her name, but I remember her art lessons in the very top class room. Our room had safety bars at the windows and looked out into the branches and leaves of the great horse-chestnut tree in the gardens of Winckley Square. The tree was huge and in its leafy foliage perched a sleepy brown owl. The bird seemed so privately mysterious and exotic to us as we peered at him from our classroom.

We had Holman Hunt's 'Scapegoat' on the walls, and a depressing picture called 'Hope', showing a lady blindfolded and plucking upon a one-stringed instrument. But these gloomy paintings could not spoil the fun of the painting lessons ... 'Left, right, take some more colour', we had to intone as we were instructed in the art of laying down a wash. (I still mutter that today ... sixty years on). I remember that once when I had forgotten my hanky and asked Miss Whiteing if I might borrow a piece of paint-rag, she lent me a dainty lace-trimmed handkerchief. How very carefully did I wash and iron this and wrap it in white tissue-paper for its return. This was not given the indignity of my knicker-leg. I suppose that the dainty piece of fine cambric, lace-trimmed, was symbolic of the difference between itself and the Grimshaw Street paint-rag like quality of earlier school-life. Our new values were now being developed like our aspirations towards finer things and a gentler scholarship.

But to be fair, we all owed such a lot to both types of school for the dedication shown by the teachers, always more important than the bricks and mortar of a school building. I recall that in that particular form we were of an age to wonder just a bit about sex, and when one girl informed us that her mother had just given birth to a baby boy we huddled together to discuss how someone so OLD could bring about such a miracle. There was certainly no sex education then, we were not allowed to walk with boys in the streets. But at the Winckley Square Junior School on Saturday mornings there was a special class for religious instruction, and ... novelty of novelties, boys from the Grammar School were able to attend. We thought this a great treat. The vicar who instructed us was unusual, too, in that he wore grey, a 'salt and pepper' tweed suit, instead of the customary black. He made us laugh, too, always a happy trait in any teacher ... what fun he was, and I passed 'The Archbishop's Exam' with flying colours ... but then, I attended church twice on Sundays each week, plus Sunday School, as did most of us in those times, when Sunday was a day apart.

Winckley Square was elegant in the early thirties. The central garden was private and surrounded by heavy iron railings. Gates were padlocked, and had to be unlocked for us to enter to play a strange game called Stool ball, a cross between cricket and rounders. We used bats larger but similar to table tennis bats and the wicket was like a notice board on a stand. I don't think it took on, and I'm not surprised. It felt 'special' to be able to sit about under the trees, for it was so lushly green and peaceful, and rhododendrons in full bloom made a lovely sight.

In the quiet square, the porches, with their iron boot-scrapers and vestibules, were almost as big as the little houses in the workaday streets we had passed along to our earlier Elementary Schools. How peaceful seemed the area with its statue of Sir Robert Peel. It is remembered as a place where nuns walked in pairs, black or grey habited. Priests in broad brimmed black hats strolled along, eyes downcast to their breviaries, for there were convents nearby and St. Wilfred's great church.

There was a special dignity about the place and it was easy to imagine that gentlefolk with carriage and pairs had dwelt there in the past. Some Suffragettes had lived there and pioneered their cause. We had been told that some of them had instigated the tarring and feathering of the Earl of Derby's statue in nearby Miller Park. Opponents to their cause had ostracised the brave women. I hope their ghosts are happy should they return to the square now, for it has been restored well.

Sadly, to me, my old school there smelled and sounded so different when I entered its doors, to look, a year or so ago. I believe now it is Preston College, and it was Tuson College when I saw it last. It seemed so utilitarian; the curtains and blinds were higgledy piggledy then, it smelled of wet macs and school dinners, and I had not the heart to ask permission to venture further than the hallway. Perhaps it was because I have such personal and treasured thoughts of the old place, good old nostalgia bothering me. Perhaps another time. Coming up to date, there are now new railings around the gardens, open to everyone. The railings which were there when I was a girl were taken down for the war effort, their iron melted down and used to keep out an invasion far more sinister than that of Preston's hoi poloi of yesteryear. How delightful, in the 1990s, to see children playing freely where once we girls of long ago felt privileged to enjoy the confines of Winckley Square Gardens.

One custom which we new girls had to learn then was that we HAD to contribute to several charities or to missions abroad. Should we forget to bring our pennies (some rich girls brought whole sixpences!) we were reminded. My mother recalled that I would plead ... 'but I HAVE to have it' when her own purse might be very slim indeed.

We also had to make 'Charity Garments' — some were more lovely than others. I remember one girl taking along beautiful hand-embroidered clothes which her grandmother had helped her with. I fear mine were made from a yard or so of flannel bought on Preston market ... they were magyar style of necessity, little nighties for little kids of narrow girth. I can still hear the squeak of the needle as it entered the thickish damp-feeling material. I shed many little drops of blood. The Sleeping Beauty's mother had nothing on me when it came to pricked fingers.

In 1930 I was lucky to have as a friend Dorothy Berry, the daughter of the caretaker at Winckley Square. This led to many treats in the school holidays. We were allowed the run of most of the school before it was cleaned and polished afresh for the coming term. We also could use the tennis court. We had fun with the speaking tubes which ran from upper to lower floors, used to summon servants previously, in the days when it was Miller Mansion. We operated the bell pulls which set the little bells in their glass case ringing in the cook's large kitchen.

There was a wine cellar, great for playing hide and seek, with its wine-bins and stillaged barrels. During the Second World War it was used as an air-raid shelter, and in 1939 some of the Grammar School boys attended our small school because of this, until their own shelter was built.

Dorothy could play the school piano by ear and her father did not mind if a few of their friends' sons shared our adventures. In the oak-panelled hall the rafters rang with brigher sounds than those heard in Assembly and the Laughing Cavalier must have felt more at home amidst all the jollity. Dorothy could bake cakes lighter than feathers in the old-fashioned kitchen, with its great scrubbed table. The only disharmony came from a bad-tempered parrot who squawked disapproval at us, and especially it hated Dorothy's red hair and often attacked her.

We drank gallons of Camp coffee, made with milk, during the hols. How innocent were those golden days — a few young boys and girls, tennis in the sun, picnics on the grass, cakes and lemonade in abundance.

Childhood, girlhood, was drawing to a close. Within a decade, those carefree boys would be soldiers, or airmen or sailors, and some would not live to see Winckley Square as it is today in Guild year of 1992. But we who are alive today remember them, and always will.

Looking back, I recall that it felt very special to be able to enter what was the teachers' sitting-room, and also to use the toilet close by which had a boxed-in lavatory with a very wide mahogany seat. This special stolen privilege gave us an exciting feeling of trespass.

When we played tennis or netball, the dentist, who had his superior type of surgery next door with its Chinese vases and goldfish tank, would watch us from his window or garden. We thought him an old man because he was going bald. He must have been all of thirty! A surgery such as his was an innovation in those days, especially to a girl like me who had suffered so much at the hands of the school dentist in his eyrie in Miller Arcade. A Winckley Square dentist was considered to be quite 'posh' ... even so, I recall that he, as well as doctors in the square at that time, had collectors who visited houses on Friday nights to collect quite tiny installments for professional work done before the days of the Health Service (Good old days!). Well, those days are long gone, but I must pay tribute to the marvellous teachers of long ago who taught us so many good values. Especially do I remember our headmistress, Miss Kathleen M. Reynolds. I even remember her very first morning assembly. She wore dark green, whereas the last headmistress, Miss Stoneman, always wore black. When Miss Reynolds smiled, her whole face lit up. She lighted a lot of love in us for many things educational, and for other important things in the lives of many of us who remember her today.

She taught us that 'Courtesy is consideration for others', and if I go to the theatre today, I sit ramrod still and do not move my head about, for Miss Reynolds warned us of this, so as not to inconvenience others sitting behind. What a little thing to remember for years but, not as the poet would have it ... 'to remember with tears'. Only with gratitude that I was a 'Winckle' ... and from this old girl (in more ways than one) ... 'Thanks for the memory'.

Sixty Years On

Old boys from Harrow sing of being 'Forty Years On, growing older and older, shorter in breath, as in memory long'. Well, in October, 1990, it was sixty years on since I was a twelve-year-old 'Scholarship Girl' about to enter the Junior Park School in Winckley Square, Preston, and now I was standing in front of my old school, which is now named as 'Preston College'.

The song continues ... 'Feeble of foot, and rheumatic of shoulder, What will it help you that once you were strong?' Well, I'll tell you something ... I don't, thank God, feel any of those sentiments. It must have something to do with my tough Lancashire upbringing of the desperate years ...

This was a sentimental journey, to be taken with many a backward glance, to those times when it seemed such a privilege to belong to a new world and totally different atmosphere from an elementary school such as Grimshaw Street School. That was a school which was one of flagged floors (and a playground paved with many gravestones) where teachers had toiled with dedication to train the pupils who came from working class homes in order that they may earn a scholarship.

That was then ... this was now, and I climbed the front steps of the porch hesitantly and reflected that long ago we girls of slender means and skinny legs, in their long black woollen stockings, never saw this door open, for the entry had been at the back, through a cobbled yard where the old stables had been. For what had been the Miller Mansion most certainly had, as all Winckley Square houses would have had, an entrance for the gentry, and one for the hoi-poi.

On this lovely autumn morning 1990, I asked permission to look around, explaining my interest to a lady who was in what had been the second form and which now was a nicely appointed restaurant. Delicious cooking smells came from where once was the old-fashioned kitchen. There, as a girl, and as a friend of the cook's daughter, I had eaten many a meal at the great scrubbed kitchen table.

In the front hall, blue and white tiled, the remembered stained glass windows are still in the staircase, only a pane or two missing; I had a great desire to slide down the bannisters, as I had done sixty years ago. I wonder what the pupils milling about there would have said to see this granny hurtling down.

The flannel bloomers of the thirties made sliding a possibility, but only to be undertaken in the hols ... when I was lucky enough to be there.

But ... back to today. 'Someone's nicked the clock!' I heard a young voice say as he glanced up at the high wall of the hall. The ghost of Miss Mary Bonney stood by me at this juncture, a lady who insisted that we spoke correctly at all times. I fancied that other teachers, some with double-barrelled names, and all single ladies, might have blanched to see pupils of today, and of both sexes holding hands and being nicely friendly together and actually running upstairs. We were not allowed to run, and seldom allowed even to use the shallow front stone stairs; mostly we used the servants' staircase at the back ... different times indeed! There was no noisy bustle in the school then. We moved around in crocodile, keeping to the left. Now there was a cheerful, busy feel about the place; pupils of different ages and nationalities milled about. There was a bar where once had been the teachers' sitting room overlooking the square (I wished it had been open, what a pleasure it would have been, to have a gin and tonic in what had been a hallowed room to us shy girls of long ago ... Some other time, perhaps!).

As I climbed the staircase, I noticed that the steps which, in my youth, had been smooth and even, were now worn and flaky (a bit like me, really) ... NO, I tell a lie, I actually felt like bounding up those stairs to my old form room at the very top of the house ... what would I find? Would the oak door still have its lovely brass knob? Would the ceiling be ornate? Would I be able to see the great horse-chestnut tree at the corner of the square where the brown owl had roosted? The tree had been planted by the Millers for a beloved son.

On my way up, and calling in at the common room, kind youngsters asked could they help me, and a courteous tutor gave me some of his precious time.

In my old classroom, a group of beefy good-looking men were having a talk on Trade Unions, and we wondered together what Thomas Miller, the first owner of the place, would have thought of that!

'May I look out of your window?' I asked ... and there was the chestnut tree; true, it had had a short back and sides ... 'Pollarded, Kathlyn' in imagination I heard Miss Whiteing, my old form-mistress, say. My feelings were very mixed and I stood there, now a granny in my seventies (with grandchildren at universities), remembering the child of twelve with her life before her.

I longed to see the tennis court where we had played on summer days in the thirties and where we had drunk lemonade under the trees. The kind man who helped me took me to a window where I could look down at the overgrown area where once we played and sported, and it looked very sad and neglected; proof, I suppose, of the stringencies in education today. I noted that some of the lovely fireplaces had been emulsioned over — that made me sad, also.

It would have perfectly rounded off my little visit had I been able to see the beamed hall which had been panelled and oak-floored in my old days. Unfortunately, there was a life class in session, so that was not possible.

Out into the sunshine, then, picking my way carefully over the still cobbled yard where once there was only the headmistress's car, which was an object of much interest way back in '29. I am easily moved to tears and yet, strangely, I felt happy after my visit and was glad to have been able to see so much of the old place.

To see Preston on a lovely morning was a delightful treat. To see Preston on a later Sunday morning, when all the main streets of the town were litter-free and perfectly clean, was a pleasure.

★ ★ ★ ★ ★

Then, to approach Preston on train travelling over the Union Railway Bridge over the River Ribble, and to see the wide river below, the sunlit fields alongside with their herds of grazing cows, took me back to my twenties childhood. Would the little wooden hut by the Tram Road still be there, where Sunday strollers of long ago could buy ice-cream served up in glass shell-shaped dishes, and where the town's mashers could hope to 'click' wiht a Sunday-best dressed flapper?

From the train I could see the tops of the great avenue of trees which flanked the old Tram Road. I wondered if bluebells and onion flowers still bloomed there in the lush grass at the sides, and where it was very damp where little streams flowed in the hollows. Sometimes the smell of the wild garlic was strong upon the balmy air when lovers had crushed them as they dallied in the springtime when many 'A young man's fancy lightly turned to thoughts of love'. And, may I add, many a young girl's, too. I know, for I was there ... half a century ago!

But this was 1990. I tried not to let my mind dwell on the Tram Bridge, where James and I became engaged so very long ago. Now, alone, the lovely lush scene was almost heart-stopping and had to be dismissed for the walk through the streets of my home town. But the ghosts, the many ghosts, tagged along with me, persistently; and who knows, maybe some of them still haunt the places here they were happy as well as sad in this Lancashire town on the banks of the Ribble.

These ghosts nudged me gently as I strolled the quiet street. I was brought to a halt outside Fishergate Baptist Chapel where I was taken as a child to the 'Mothers' Bright Hour' there. Mothers did take their children along, reluctant children in many cases, and only the thoughts of the rich plum cake and sweet tea made up for the lengthy but cheerful hymn-singing and prayers. I recalled being envious of a little girl called Babs who always wore ribbon-bedecked straw hats and silky frilly frocks ... I envied Babs with her ringlets and shiny shoes. Babs, like me, must have reached her biblical span by now, and perhaps will be thankful. Like me.

(How sad to think that devilish forces, in the guise of human beings, should cause desecration to the chapel by planting a bomb nearby in 1991.)

The ghost of my father stood beside me as I saw that the old Lancashire Evening Post and Guardian offices were gone. Now, there is nothing left of the place ... but I do wonder what has happened to the bust of the pioneer of printing, Caxton, whose stone effigy was high up on the building.

★ ★ ★ ★ ★

In the twenties, printers were printers, and did not have fancier names, such as Linotype operators. They wore smelly, ink-stained overalls which had to be washed at home (I can smell them now!). Dad said there were 'Printer's Devils' working at the Post ... but Mother said ... 'Hush' if he said that, for 'devil' was a naughty word which we were not allowed to say in those long-gone days. I remember that when there was a song about Anne Boleyn who 'Walked the Bloody Tower' my brother was banned and threatened with a thick ear should he use such bad language.

I loved to call at the paper's premises when I was a girl, perhaps to take a message to my father when he was secretary of the Typographical Association. I saw such mysteries as printing blocks and long wooden boxes holding silvery type. Christmas cards were made and printed there — cards with glitter all around their deckled edges. Printers were issued with pints of milk when working with the sparkling gold and silver dust because it had harmful properties. They also made pretty dance cards with tiny pink and blue pencils attached by thin cord. The dancers wrote their partner's names on the cards in order to claim a dance later. I can remember the feel of the heavy shiny paper used for brochures and programmes and pageants and festivals. The printing was fanciful and decorative. Illustrations had a Burne-Jones like quality and beauty. Capital letters in one pageant book (perhaps the Schools' Pageant in the twenties) were almost like those in early holy books illustrated by monks.

Sample books for Christmas cards, when finished with, were given to me to play with. I still remember the delight of turning over the large pages, stroking the smooth cards, taking tiny cards from inside silk and lace envelopes which were pasted onto the larger cards. The small cards when removed from their diminutive envelopes would have the names of the senders on them. 'From Mr. and Mrs. Jones and Emily', for example ... no first names then for married people.

On one visit to Preston, before the 'Post' offices were demolished, I did my usual pilgrimage down Fishergate. I noticed that the man selling papers had a shelter there. When it was the 'Lancashire Daily Post' I remember that the papers were placed on the wide sill of the building and that a man in a wheelchair sold them. He wore a bowler. He had a black waterproof apron on his chair, for I think he had lost his legs in the Grear War. I seemed to remember a man called 'Little Harry' who scuttled along on a wooden bogey, for he was without legs. For this was in the days before the NHS and shameful to recall that such things could be.

Yes, the offices of the paper hold a special place in my mind, for it was all part of my childhood. Particularly I do remember that my first holiday, when I went away to Blackpool for a full week, was possible because when Sir. George Toulmin, who owned the paper, died in the 20s, all the workforce was left money depending in amount upon their length of service. I was decked out in new clothes, clothes I remember to this day, and had a real holiday in Blackpool.

I remember, too, that at the funeral of Sir George the workmen walked in procession to the service, and that they all sang his favourite hymn ... 'How Sweet the Name of Jesus Sounds'. When a woman of my age can remember such things, and how my Father's employer was mourned by him, and remembered by me, there must have been something very special about the man who thought well of his workers. He, too, I'm sure, would like to know that dear old Caxton's bust is safe and well and that 127 Fishergate will not be forgotten.

The cinema in Fishergate is still there, known as the New Victoria when I was a girl, and where the mighty organ would rise up from the depths and play triumphantly whilst we bought our twopenny blocks of ice-cream and delighted in the comfort of the plush velvet seats.

I did not venture down the sunless Old Cock Yard next to the cinema — it looked too narrow and menacing. I was reminded of the New Cock Inn which had been off Fishergate and where illegal cock-fights had taken place, for when it was demolished the cock-pit was unearthed. It was remembered by me as a place of celebration on V.E. night, when it was jam-packed with soldiers, sailors and airmen, the celebration saddened by the knowledge that so many men had been sacrificed, men who should never be forgotten. Many ghosts in my Preston rememberings.

I felt terribly alone this Sabbath, and vulnerable, as widows so often do, and the sight of what appeared to be two Victorian graves with bright flowers seen through the black railings, in front of the Miller Arcade, did not help my sombre mood. But a cheery ghost came to my aid and reminded me that in days long gone the lads and lasses would meet nearby on a Sunday, after church, for the strolling through the town. Many a likely lad would raise his newly-acquired bowler or trilby hat, and many a Lancashire lass would simper under her cloche hat and be proud of her silken stockings kept just for Sundays.

Brucciani's Ice Cream Parlour in Fishergate was the venue for many of the town's lads and lasses of the thirties. It had a soda fountain and many varieties of ice cream. We never know how to pronounce this exotic-sounding Italian name, giving it the hard C treatment. As chance would have it, one of our companions was a young Swiss man, on a sort of exchange visit to Mears's shop whilst the son of that business visited Rorschach in Switzerland. Arnold Engensperger played a musical saw, wore a trilby hat and was viewed askance by the Preston lads, though we girls quite fancied him! He was anxious to grow a moustache and our lads, spitefully, told him that he must rub raw onion on his upper lip as encouragement! And the poor chap believed it.

War clouds were gathering in 1938 — ready for the September of 1939, and by then our Swiss friend had gone away, as so very soon all our group of young men was to depart, alas, not to Switzerland.

It was as well we could not know what was to come, and the next time I saw one of our cafe group — many years later he was like a living skeleton, after his stint on the Burma Railway and life as a prisoner of the Japs. But he was, at least, a living skeleton; there were many lovely lads who never saw their homes again. And, although Vera Lynn sang 'We'll meet again', it often had a very hollow ring during those tragic years of the war.

The new cinema, then the 'New Victoria' with its opulent chandeliers, was a popular meeting place before the 'parade', being so centrally situated. Merigold's shop was on one corner of Avenham Street (always alive with Bookies' runners during weekdays) and Woods' Tobacconists, with its workshop, on the other. The girls from there used to troop out all smelling of tobacco. One of my friend's sisters who worked there not only smelled of cigarettes, but had tobacco-coloured hair, all crinkly, too, just like the tobacco! Her sister worked in the Gold Thread works nearby — how lovely that sounded — and they would meet at dinner-time and, with arms linked, go home for their dinner. No works canteens then!

What else were planners doing to my old home town, I wondered. I was visiting it after several years away and I just had to go down to Winckley Square and my old Frenchwood haunts. I feared the worst. As I have a friend in Ireland who once lived in Bank Parade, I had promised to look there and report.

How pleased I was at what I found, for the last time I'd seen the square where I started my school life at the Junior Park, it had been forlorn, overgrown and all open and unprotected, full of marauding dogs and wine-sodden tramps.

I, of course, had known it as a girl as being enclosed by iron railings, dense with foliage and alive with bird-song and sometimes with schoolgirls allowed in to play a strange game called stool-ball in a small clearing. Gates were firmly padlocked then and, of course, the railings went to the war effort.

On another visit to Preston, on a Sunday in winter, a day of frost and ice, I wondered to myself if they still flooded the valley in Avenham Park when it was freezing cold. What a treat that was way back in the twenties. Those lucky enough to own ice-skates could cut an unaccustomed dash. Children who wore clogs could glide along on the periphery of the ice, trying not to get in the way of the experts. Those of us whose mothers refused to let us wear clogs, even though our thin shoes might be down-at-heel, had to make do with sliding at the very edges of the ice, where the frilled frozen edges met the crisp frozen grass on the south side of the ornate ironwork bandstand. This then stood in the centre of the valley, a proper place for a bandstand. Sometimes we wore thick woollen stockings over our shoes, better to slip easily along the ice. How I longed for the forbidden clogs, but some mothers, in those days, had a false sense of pride as many of my age will remember. My own mother, even though, at times home-soled shoes were decrepit with their little brass nails cutting into tender feet, would say — as I begged for spark-striking clogs. 'No ... you'll never wear clogs.'

So the valley, with the ice-making, a wondrous play-ground for the Preston children, and a romantic setting for the young mashers and flappers of the times, might be remembered today.

The gas-lamps along the top walks, and those by the tram bridge and along the riverbank, would be lighted by the lamp-lighter. Hot-potato carts would be waiting by the Railway Bridge in the spots used by Eldorado Ice-Cream sellers in the days of summer. The duck pond, then JUST a pond, without railings and bridge as it is today, would also be frozen over, and the ducks huddled under the laurel bushes. Older brothers and sisters, intent on a little dalliance, would try to lose us younger siblings and, as the dusk deepened and the many excited dogs skittered over the ice, barking loudly, we young ones would group together till our elders appeared, and perhaps we would be bribed with a hot potato not to 'tell Dad.'

So we would wend our way homewards, running to keep warm. Houses were not centrally heated then; the fire in the living room possibly the only warm place in the house, and therefore the centre of all family life, a welcoming, warm, glowing haven.

What better way to end my last (so far) sentimental journey than with the sound of childish laughter echoing down the years. In the mind's eye the picture of the twenties full of childish optimism, the hope of the young in heart, the faith and Lancashire gutsy spirit which, I trust, has carried so many through to the 1990s and one more Preston Guild.

The White Windsor Soap Works, Preston

In 1879, prior to the 1882 Preston Guild, Joshua Margerison, founder of the only soap-making firm in the town, and whose son William McKune Margerison was later to be elected Mayor twice, took over an old cotton mill in Leighton Street. He manufactured the famous White Windsor Soap there, which was sold all over this country and abroad. The trade mark was the round tower of Windsor Castle. Queen Victoria raised no objection to this — perhaps the soap's whiteness and purity met with the royal approval.

The aristocracy and the very rich must have used the Preston-made soap, for the Cunard White Star Line bought the soaps made by the firm for the bathrooms in their luxury liners, because it gave a good lather in the water used aboard their cruisers. Harrods and Selfridge's stocked the soaps, too.

Had Joshua started out in business at the time of the 1992 Guild, he would perhaps have qualified for a Business Enterprise Grant but, at the time of his venture, the reality was much more romantic...

The old cotton mill was not the first of the premises to be used by Joshua and his six sons, for there had been a small factory close by Marsh Lane and, more fascinating to the mind, the barn of the family farm in Hoghton had seen the experimenting with tallow for the process of soap-making. Such a use made unnecessary the boiling stage in the manufacturing of soap.

From such small beginnings developed one of Preston's important businesses. A descendant of Joshua's described to me how her own Grandpa, when a small boy, had seen Joshua, on returning from his travels, stand on one side of the farm's fireplace and throw golden guineas, one at a time, into the outstretched apron of his wife. He has asked her to sit at the other side of the fire to catch in her pinny the gleaming coins. When the little child was a grown man he still remembered how the guineas glinted as they caught the firelight. What a painting that would have made! What a piece of family history to be treasured.

The White Windsor Soap Works, Leighton Street, Preston, is no more. It was burnt down in 1948. Nearby were cottages, and at the door of Mrs. Noblett's, fifty years and more ago, larks in cages sang. They trilled so merrily as though they were ascending high into the sky, as high even as the top of the spire of the lovely St. Walburgh's steeple, which gleamed then, as now, above Preston's rooftops.

Mr. Noblett had an ice-making business, and in the summer his wife sold delicious ice-cream from a tub set on her doorstep.

'Isn't it sad to see the birds in cages?' we would ask as we bought the mouth-watering ice-cream wafers when we nipped out from the office on hot sunny days.

'They must be happy, or they wouldn't sing,' Mrs. Noblett would reply, and, doubting, we were still too unsure of ourselves at seventeen to dispute this ... times were different then!

On a corner was a newsagent's shop. The owner did a good trade in small brown envelopes. She told us that some of our workmen bought these and placed their wages (depleted by just a little for extra 'spence') in them to give to their unsuspecting wives. In actual fact, the wages were distributed from aluminium containers carried round on a large tray. The envelopes were a nicety thought up by the men!

Office staff had their pay in little envelopes, and we carefully kept the fact to ourselves if we should get a little 'rise'. We had to pluck up courage when suggesting to our superiors that we would like more. An extra half-crown a week was most welcome.

In 1936, going to work in an office was a new experience. I had no special skills except that I could type, as when I was at Preston Park School we were forbidden to take extra-mural work in case it interfered with school studies. At my interview at Margerisons' I was so nervous I forgot to put any paper in my 'sit up and beg' sort of typewriter and typed away happily on the platen until my mistake was pointed out. My face felt as bright red as the hair of Veronica the junior with whom I was to work for several years. I was soon put at ease, though, for it was that sort of place; a friendly, family atmosphere all round, indeed the owners seemed to be more like elderly uncles to us ... though in reality they would only be middle-aged!

To us they were Mr. Richard, Mr. Will, Mr. Harry and Mr. Gilbert, and when younger members of the family came along they were Master Bill, Master Douglas and Master George. This did seem slightly feudal to us as they were about the same age as we young girls, but it was just how things were in the thirties, and certainly we were quite happy as we so enjoyed working for the family, and feeling a part of it all. Sometimes daughters of the owners drove their parents to work, and this seemed extremely daring to us as, of course, there were not many lady drivers then, and not all that many cars on the roads. One of the cousins had a chauffeur-driven car (my grandfather owned a car and my brother a battered Baby Austin Seven) but I used to go to work on my bicycle, bought at half a crown a week from a shop in Cheapside, and, as I loved to speed down Leighton Street, Mr. Harry, who always walked to the office, or rather strode, swinging his ashplant walking stick, would tell me that I was sure to come to grief at the bottom of the hill. Mr. Harry never wore an overcoat. He was a Major, decorated in the Great War with the M.C. We thought him handsome with his small moustache and proud bearing, and were just a little in awe of him. The other family owners were large and well-rounded, with gold watch-chains with fobs dangling over their well-tailored waistcoats.

To any office worker of the nineties, used to a high-tech environment, with photo-copiers, fax machines and word-processors, our cosy offices and equipment would seem like something from the Antiques Road Show.

We had turkey-red carpets, coal fires, Windsor chairs which were padded with cushions, and some high Dickensian desks with very high stools which were used when ledger-work was done. The windows were small-paned. Letters were weighed on a small brass balance, typed letters or invoices were placed between the parchment-coloured dampened thin silky pages of a big red book. Then the book was placed in a press, a great screw was turned to force an iron plate down onto the book, so that the letters were thus copied and their imprint remained in the book for later reference.

This ancient equipment was in the typist's office next to our general office and the girls there worked on a huge oval polished mahogany table. The picture of the founder of the firm, Joshua Margerison, looked down sternly from the wall. He had been a local Methodist preacher and would perhaps have been not quite at home at dinner-times in that particular room. For then the typewriters were cleared away and the room was used for dining by the owners, who were his grandsons, and very well they dined, too. For we had our own cook at the firm, Gladys, who had her flagged kitchen with its great iron fireplace and scrubbed wooden table down below. The smell of roasting Scotch Beef, which was delivered from Scotland, wafted down the corridor at dinner-times, its gorgeous mouth-watering smell competing with the scent (which was not quite a scent) of the famous White Windsor Soap.

Later, the room would have the rich aroma of pipe and cigar smoke, and the inn-like atmosphere would surely have been anathema to the founder, but we girls loved it, for it added to the pleasure of working at the Soap Work. We would sniff the air like Bisto kids and liked to go into the typists' room where one of the ladies had a very haughty and queenly bearing, and whose handsome bust we skinny ones admired greatly.

There was a small wooden telephone exchange on the desk in our General Office, about the size of a small suitcase. It had pegs and a row of what looked like grey eyeballs with lids which came down to cover them when the 'phone rang. We had several extensions to the works and other offices, and I was terrified of it at first, for I often connected the wrong people or cut them off altogether. Each night before I went to sleep, I would practise in my mind thus . . . 'If number three eyelid goes down and Mr. Gilbert wants Mr. Richard, I must crank the handle after putting Mr. G's peg to the level position . . . then I must depress both pegs at the same angle', and so on. I had nightmares until I mastered this ancient and tricky device.

Some workpeople were afraid of the telephone, for in those days they were not in common use. One foreman, Fred Turner, who always wore a flat cap and white apron at work, would never answer his 'phone, and unless Florrie or Ted answered for him it meant a trip into the works to take any message to him. This could be harzardous, as the floors were greasy; stairs sometimes of wood and sometimes of iron, and fairly steep, were hard to negotiate in high-heeled shoes. I loved court shoes and would save up the Eight Shillings and Elevenpence for a pair of Timpson's, which I had to take off to climb the iron narrow steps, which were like gratings and dangerous to high heels. As my wage was Fifteen Shillings a week for a five-and-a-half-day week, I was not exactly flush for cash.

On Saturday mornings we went to work in our 'Sunday Best', wearing our church-going hats. How we kept up appearances I can't imagine, but one of our office staff had a rabbit-fur coat which we all envied. On Saturday mornings we muttered to each other that her parents must be well-off!

Just to point out the different customs of those times, Veronica's grandmother had died, so for a full six months Veronica came to work in a black dress. When the six months was up, she arrived at the office one day in a lavender dress with a pale green chiffon scarf at the neck. With her flame-coloured hair, she was a delight to the eye after seeing her so long dressed in mourning. I remember thinking that she looked like a breath of spring.

Unlike a breath of spring was the tallow room. We did not like to go into the room, for it did not smell very nice, and when in the works we skirted the vats which I think held caustic soda, for we had been told by workmen that stray cats were often found dead in them, and we were horrified. Another feature of the works was a brass steam kettle used for 'brewing up' for workmen who used white enamel brew-cans. This steam kettle always seemed to send forth a stream of hissing steam and an eldrich shriek just as one passed by. So what with walking gingerly because of the slippery floors and jumping nervously when the kettle gave forth, the works could be an intimidating place.

The cobbled yard, especially on icy days, was treacherous, and it was nice to get back to our very cosy and warm office. On the days when ice formed on the nearby canal and it was very cold, only then did Mr. Harry acknowledge it was wintry. Still no overcoat, but he had little grey knitted cuffs which matched his tweed jacket and grey flannel trousers. He told us that the cuffs kept the body heat up! On such days, Mr. Richard would warm the satin lining of his overcoat in front of our roaring fire before venturing out to car or taxi-cab.

On a day when the canal was not frozen over, we had a small drama. A little lad, his face as white as our soap, and his eyes staring, thumped on our office door ... 'Please Miss, me brother's fell in't' canal and he's gone down THREE times!' Why he stayed to count I'll never know, but Bill, who was in our office at the time, dashed out and rescued the little chap from a watery death. I expect they were both glad of our strong carbolic soap, for canals are not exactly trout streams.

In the 1922 procession, Margerison's Soap Works exhibited, on a float, a five-and-a-half ton replica in White Windsor Soap of Windsor Castle. There were busts, too, of Queen Victoria and Prince Albert.

A Preston man has told me that his grandfather's firm made the moulds for Margerisons. The mould, for the castle tower, and those of the queen and her consort, had to be oiled before being filled. Apprentices from Preston Fibrous Plasterers vied with each other for this task. This was because the girls who worked in the soap works, on hot days, wore flimsy frocks! Lads never change!

They also had the firm's name worked in coloured toilet soaps surrounding Preston's coat of arms ... all in carved soap! I'm told that in the official Guild Guide of 1922, Margerisons' soaps were stated to be 'the finest soap in the world for all household purposes'. Their Marcura Shaving Soap was claimed to be 'superior to anything made either in this country or abroad'. Modesty was not, apparently, to be a part of advertising then, but then it never is!

In the 1902 Guild the firm had a tableau depicting a 'dirty little boy' being scrubbed clean with the firm's soap. His descendents were told that he was exceedingly cross at having such an ignominious role. Stories handed down by families are to be treasured.

In my time at the firm in the late thirties, we girls were asked for suggestions for names when new lines in soaps, perfumes or bath salts or bath cubes came out. The old names took a bit of beating, though ... Peach Bloom, Honeysuckle, Babeskin, Glycerine and Cucumber, Orange Blossom, to name but a few. I seem to recall that there was also a soap which floated in the bath, but I think it was rather speckled with oatmeal and a bit 'grainy' to use ... but little children loved it!

One Christmas, just before the war, we were shown samples of pretty little bottles, bright gold and silvery papers for covering the little gift boxes, and asked to select patterns and also names for new perfumes. We thought 'Temptation' and 'Desire' might make a nice change. These names were not used, and I'm sure the founder, Joshua Margerison, of the stern countenance, would certainly not have approved.

Soon, family businesses will be rare, but in the thirties, in Lancashire, I expect there were quite a few firms like Margerison's where all the employees felt as though they belonged, and that owners took a genuinely fatherly interest in all who worked for them. When the war came and because soap-making was an essential industry, we were not called up, but had to do voluntary work. We were often tired in the office from doing all-night duty at the Police switchboard, which was in the basement of the then new Municipal Building in Lancaster Road. When on night duty, we slept in the Mayor's parlour, which had a lovely blue carpet. We had blue blankets on our fold-up beds and should there be a red alert had to shoot down below to man the 'phones. We girls from Margerison's also did duty at the Fire Station in Tithebarn Street ... and learned to shin down a brass pole (a skill not since needed!). Preston Station all-night buffet saw us, too, dishing out mugs of tea to soldiers and airmen on Troop trains.

I am sure I have the distinction of being the only war-time girl to have had a packet of best butter rubbed on her legs on Preston Station! An army sergeant from the Catering Corps performed the task to the tune of many wolf whistles. As I carried a bucket of scalding tea, I was felled by a dashing soldier, I was drenched, but the 'first aid' proved effective.

For some reason when training at the fire station, we were instructed always to carry string and scissors in our pockets in case we met any lady about to give birth. All I can say is thank heaven this encounter never arose. I can remember that we would walk home in the black-out, often alone after a night-shift, sometimes with sirens wailing, praying that no lady in the perilous state of partuition would cross our path! Voluntary work kept us all very busy, but at least we were safe at home.

Not so one of the Margerisons ... Bill, who was a prisoner of war of the Germans. When it was known that he was at least a prisoner and not killed, one of the older women workers in the factory bought bottles of wine for us to celebrate. Unfortunately, she didn't tell us that she was teetotal and that the 'wine' was of the tonic variety, full of phosphates and quite ghastly to drink. She poured quite large amounts and we had to get through it trying to keep our faces straight and our lips from pleating up.

Still, she meant well, and we were all glad that Mr. Will's son was safe. One day we got a strangely addressed postcard at the office ... Mr. I. N. C. Hains, Margerison's Soap Works, Preston, was the address. After much puzzling over this, there being no such workman there, some clever person deciphered it as meaning that some German prisoners were in chains. The Red Cross was alerted, needless to say.

I well remember in wartime seeing an elderly bowler-hatted 'Traveller' (we didn't call them 'Reps' then) who had been recalled to work for the firm. He was making his way painfully over the cobbles in the yard, his little cardboard box holding his obligatory gas-mask, slung over his overcoated shoulder with string. I felt so dreadfully sad; he looked so pathetic and tired, and, though I was only twenty then, I really grieved to think that we, all of us, were at war.

They were unhappy times, and on November 11th all the works would gather for two minutes' silence, and when we thought of boys we knew, and brothers and fathers who were away, and also of Mr. Will's son, we all cried when his father recited Binyon's poem ... 'At the going down of the sun ... we will remember them'.

The works which was famous for the White Windsor Soap burnt down, oddly enough on November 5th, 1948. It was at dinner-time, so all the huge ledgers were out of the safes and on the high Dickensian desks, so records were lost. It was a great blaze, for the ingredients for soap manufacturing would fuel the flames well.

A younger member of the family, George, was walking down Friargate in the dinner-time break. He smelled smoke, saw the glow in the sky, and a piece of burnt paper fluttered down to land at his feet. He saw part of the ornate printing of the familiar letter-head, and knew, before he started running, what he would find.

Thus came to an end the old factory which had produced the famous White Windsor Soap from 1868 to 1948, and whose products featured in several Preston Guilds ... but not, alas, in this one of 1992. Except, perhaps, and maybe in photographs of past Guilds produced to delight the many Prestonians who like to look back sometimes at Preston's past and those who helped to shape it, and who should be remembered.

The Home Fires

My Rochdale supermarket has strange and exotic food for sale, rare fruits and spices, foreign dishes for the epicurean, pre-packed and frozen foods at one time unknown to Lancashire tastes. Such delicacies as quails' eggs are available to tempt a Lancashire palate. Our children and grandchildren know the names of Italian dishes as well as we older ones knew about trotters, black puddings, oatcakes, duckamuffins and sheeps' brains way back in the 1920s and 1930s.

But one display in our newest supermarket had me puzzled, as well as my grand-daughter ... and yet it was something we all bought for a penny, rough and ready, tied up in bundles, often hawked about the streets by little children in their home-made orange-boxes on wheels, a necessity of life, giver of warmth, when the fireside was the very centre of home life rather than the bright box in the corner.

My grand-daughter (who has never seen a poker, or an open fire, or a bag of soot) asked what the neat plastic bags, filled with what she thought were sticks of celery, so white and uniform they were, were used for. I had to examine them myself quite closely to see that the bags were indeed bags of firewood, but not firewood as we recognise. These white sticks, of uniform size, packed into clear plastic bags, bore no resemblance to the rough and ready grainy sticks, often misshapen because of knot-holes, splintery and smelly, and often dirty and rough-hewn. Those bundles, tied up with twisted wire, would never have been given shelf-room in a modern shop.

In the old days, the bundles were consigned to the back room of many a Co-op, along with vinegar barrels, the candles, the paraffin drums and the mothball-smelling packets of firelighters. In small shops the rough-trade firewood bundles were stacked on the flagged floor in close proximity, with the hard red blocks of carbolic soap, the tins of grate-polish and the little bags of coals.

In war-time paper bags of stout quality bulged with dusty ovoids, those pathetic excuses for real coal. Oh yes, firewood had a distinctive smell, then compounded of the smells of its humble companions. Firewood bundles bore no resemblance to the sanitised, refined and trimmed, machine-sliced kindling on sale now. No, this white pre-packed, plastic-wrapped commodity, like so many instant comestibles, was ready for instant use by the kindling-users of today. There would be no need to protect the hands from the oily feel and smell of the bundled wood, which we had to store separately; no need to wield an axe, as we attacked the chunky wood to make it go further by splitting the sticks. Pensioners of today must recall what a struggle it was when a knot was lurking in the sticks, how the axe would judder and baulk in protest.

Present-day children must hear and be thankful that they do not have to work so hard to help a parent to prepare for the basic necessity of a warm room, as we did when only one room in a humble, and not-so-humble, home, was the only heated room. But then they cannot know what a treat it was to cuddle up close to a blazing hearth on a cold winter's night, listening to the magic of wireless, using the imagination to picture far-off entertainment, and so see close at hand the pictures in the fire, the flaming grottoes, the imagined castles, the sparks flying up the black sooty chimney.

Then if a child fell ill, a parent would take a shovelful of flaming coals up to a bedroom's tiny iron fireplace, and it was luxury indeed to watch the shadows on the ceiling in a warm bed, which had been heated by the oven-shelf from the fireside oven, or by a hot house-brick wrapped round with flannel. Only we who are today's pensioners will recall as children bathing in a zinc bath by a fireside screened by the clothes-maiden draped with towels for privacy. These are simple remembered pleasures of a childhood which was never affluent.

As we grew up and had home of our own in wartime, even a coal fire was often a luxury; carts selling peat were to be seen in towns, as they had been seen during the 1926 coal strike. How sullenly it burned, needing many a prod with a poker. My grand-daughter, as I said, does not know what a poker is, and I had to explain what it was when telling the tale of Goldilocks and the Father Bear brandishing the poker as she fled. There was another use for a heavy poker when folks lived in back-to-back houses, or even semi-detached ones. Quarrelling neighbours could be quelled by the judicious rattling of a poker on the chimney back.

A child may expect Father Christmas to come down the chimney and for his robes to remain soot-free. But one Whitsuntide we had an unexpected visitor down our chimney, bringing down a whole carpetful of soot and covering my daughter, who was dressed ready for the Whit walk in snowy white, in a pall of soot.

At our front door was a small urchin asking 'Please can we have our pigeon back?' We looked like black and white minstrels, but the bird, pigeon-toed, hot-footing it on our coals, was in a sorry state. Red-eyed to start with, and getting more so by the minute, it waddled across the blackened carpet and perched on the bookshelf. It took a year before every book's pages were really clean. It also took us most of that Whit Monday to clean up.

The sackful of soot we collected was dumped at the back of our garden, and a week later my smallest son, with his tiny girlfriend, presented themselves at the back door, covered from head to toe in black soot. 'We've been playing at being chimney sweeps', they cried, joyfully. We no longer see sweeps about, and I'm not sorry when I think of the stuff.

It is nice to remember the roasted chestnuts, the cosiness of the fires, those exciting little spurts of blue flame which used to erupt when one could afford best shiny black coal ... which wasn't often! But most of us were glad to rid ourselves of the fire-irons, the fenders, the cow-rakes for the ashes, the damper-irons, the sheets of enamel painted like tiles to imitate a tiled hearth, along with the coal-buckets and the need for a chimney-sweep. (Yet, last week I saw advertised in a posh magazine brass fenders for sale).

Many of us who are grandparents now must recall with horror how we sometimes had to take the baby's pram along to the gas works to plead for coke to keep the home fires burning way back in the 1940s.

Old customs die out, along with those words which were commonplace to Lancashire folk. Who but ourselves would know what an 'Ess oyl' was, that dusty space under an oven or a fire-back where the ashes fell, and from whence they had to be removed with a small shovel, which grated horribly on the rough surface? The cow-rake came in handy then.

Who today would know what a 'blower' is? They will not have had the experience of holding the tinny sheet with its jutting handle up against a fire as an encouragement for it to get going. How many sheets of the Chronicle must have been set alight in Oldham as they were plastered up against the metal as further encouragement to a sulky fire?

On cold days, when the crofts and brews were icy, blowers, oven-shelves and even enamel hearths were used as makeshift slides and toboggans. On such cold days, children without gloves would stuff a mustard tin with cotton-waste, set it alight and, when the tin was hot, it was used as a hand-warmer, or a winter-warmer. You can buy their descendants at Harrods or at huntin', shootin'and fishin' shops. My late husband was given one as a present. It was made of stainless steel, leather-bound, and was fuelled by little sticks of methylated substance. It was in a red velvet covering — a far cry from the little mustard tins of yesteryear.

Monkey Runs

In the cotton towns of the twenties and thirties, to my certain knowledge, for I was there, so that youngsters could meet and mingle with the opposite sex, 'Monkey Runs' were commonplace. Each town had its recognised streets or venues where they could parade. On summer evenings especially, and more particularly on Sunday evenings (after church or chapel) the lads and lasses of the towns would stroll in twos and threes hoping to 'click', 'trap off' or maybe just catch the eye of one of the other strollers whom they might fancy.

The girls would glance sideways at the 'mashers' who passed nonchalently by, weighing up form. All the lasses could dream of being as attractive and desirable as their idols of the silver screen. Mary Pickford with her curls, Pola Negri with her sultry gypsy looks, or Clara Bow ... the 'It' Girl. They, the girls, mostly aspired to having 'It' or 'Oomph' ... whatever that might mean! But if the girls had either, the chaps would soon know. One thing all had in common was the old-age desire to attract. Why else would they dress up to the nines, the girls secretly using the prohibited make-up? Many a Prestonian must have met their partner-for-life, perhaps in the many Temperance Bars of the town, perhaps in the little 'Hut' just over the Old Tram Bridge, Preston, maybe in Jackson's Cafe in Church Street, or, in the thirties, in Bruccianni's in Fishergate ... the latter being my happy hunting ground then. When that particular shop was new and exciting to us youngsters ... it was considered quite 'posh', so different from the wooden hut where we would drink VIMTO ... sometimes hot, other times cold. Sarsaparilla, Dandelion and Burdock made by Seeds or Attwaters, or ice-cream served up in little glass shells.

Because Prestonians will read this (I hope) and many of them may have memories as long as mine, here are a few of the places recalled where the Vimto and Sodas and ice-creams were consumed, often by customers who sat on little wooden benches which were ranged along the wall inside the little house-shop in Avenham Lane. There, because it was a herbal shop, you could also buy herbal tobacco to be smoked in a little brown glazed pipe, or even a clay-pipe. What sophisticates the lads felt themselves to be as they puffed away.

In the little hut just across the Old Tram Bridge, we sat at little tables; the chairs were the sort which circled the bandstand when it was in the middle of the 'Valley' in Avenham Park. On Sundays, after a stroll in the park, all the flappers and mashers visited the little hut, and if it happened to be a warm night the proprietor put little tables and chairs outside, so that, what with the view of the Ribble and the nearby lovely Old Tram Road, there was a kind of magic about, to be treasured in memory by those of us who are today's grandparents. The 'Continental', near Broadgate, was for the more affluent strollers.

Jackson's Cafe in Church Street served ice-cream with fresh cream on top for sixpence, a real treat, and for which I wheeled out many a Preston baby to earn the necessary cash. I remember well how I dressed when older and able to spend just a little more in Bruccianni's before the war.

Old photographs may show what our twenties flappers looked like, and a description may amuse those who never saw them in their full and fascinating flesh ...

I was not a flapper of the twenties; my salad days came later in the thirties and I remember them well! But I can recall how my elder sister dressed and behaved, probably the same as any other Oldham or Preston girl of the times, who found life on highdays and holidays marvellous and thrilling and romantic filtering through the textile-mill haze of their own cotton town.

The desire to be beautiful meant that they had to apply their cosmetics secretly and only after the attendance at the chapel, then it was removed with spit on a hanky before going home to a parent who might ask 'what time to you call this' if the clock showed anything after ten. Lipstick was not used freely, except by 'fast' girls. Tangee or Kissproof lipstick were yet to come. Little 'poudre-papiers' had to be kept hidden in a clutch-bag out of sight of parents. A few girls plucked their eyebrows into a narrow line and sometimes used a pencil to darken it, but my mother disapproved of any form of make-up at all and my sister had to hide her twopenny tins of Snowfire powder away. One day her secret box was found. I remember well the tiny silvery tin which had a screw top lid whose thread would get crossed and make impossible to open. I would struggle to open such a box just to smell the powder and experiment. Unfortunately, when Mother found Elsie's little box it was thrown on the fire. I can see it now, burning to a brilliant red as it glowed on the coals and disintegrated ... 'A temptation of the Devil,' said my chapel-going parent ... I thought Old Nick was getting his own back. Elsie cried!

I can only speak about the girls of Preston of sixty years ago, but my elder sister was a flapper of the twenties, as I have said. But my husband, who was a 'masher' of the twenties also, could tell me of how the hopeful lads dressed, emulating such idols as Rudolph Valentino, that sleepy-eyed incredibly handsome toreador hero of 'Blood and Sand' or as the masterful, irresistible 'Sheik of Araby' ... he was every girl's romantic starlit dream.

In imitation of Ramon Navarro, who was anoher scintillating star of the times, many youthful heads were smoothed to a patent-leather glossy blackness ... a prerequisite for Latin Lovers. A few youths would wave their hair with their sister's curling tongs, or even blacken their budding little moustaches with an eyebrow pencil. They would attempt sideburns just like Rudolph's.

So the young hopefuls would parade the streets. Fishergate was one venue, and I'm told that Friargate was for the younger girls and boys, not yet welcome to join their elders, but just as anxious to 'show off'. It was ever thus ... and so it is with dress today, though today it is called ... 'Making a statement' ... which one would think meant being individualistic, but actually means the young ones don a kind of uniform ... but still in imitation of their idols. (I note that my grand-daughter often looks like Max Wall ... I dread the time when teenagers might discover Frank Randle with his hiking shorts and skinhead wig ... for then we really will see some sights! Not that we don't today ... How the youngsters of today would hoot with laughter had they seen us in our salad days. The Oxford Bags, the Plus Fours, the spats and waistcoats, the bowler hats and trilbies of the chaps would surely send them into hysterics.

The girls of the cotton towns' Monkey Parades, in their finery, would look mostly alike, striving to be fashionable for all to see. Dresses would be low-waisted, stockings silk or lisle and seamed. Hats were obligatory, often home-made, a 'shape' being bought and then covered and beribboned or befeathered. Shoes, low or louis heeled, worn instead of the clogs which mill girls wore on weekdays, must have made a welcome change, their unaccustomed lightness perhaps lightening the spirit, too.

Today's bikini-knickered girls would hoot with laughter if they could see the directoire knickers, elasticated at knee-level and waist, which their forebears wore (the lasses, that is!). Because frocks were fairly short in the twenties, there was always a danger that if a knicker-elastic broke and a safety pin not handy, the offending 'leg' had to be tucked up out of sight, always in danger of descending to embarrass the wearer. Cami-knickers were in vogue a few years later and very draughty they were, too, the buttons always coming unfastened.

Corsets were mostly worn by older women, but the girls on the lookout for likely lads probably wore the elastic body-belts, forerunners of the two-way stretch. But the girls who must have been eyed hopefully and perhaps with dalliance aforethought were the ones who jiggled as they walked, and some fast-cats even wore garters with tiny bells on them, tinkling forth who knows what promise of pneumatic bliss ... (or was sex only discovered in the sixties?).

Such an invitation must surely have many a masher to nudge a fellow masher with the joyful aside from the corner of the mouth and a lascivious mutter of 'EH OOP LADS!'

Generation Gap

My grandchildren often stay with me and on two bedroom doors there are little notices. One reads 'Helen's Room ... only James Band fans admitted'. The other one says 'Alison and Junior's Room. No admittance if you don't like Michael Jackson'. (I might add that Junior is a fanged and horned monster, even though a cuddly one. Children have such strange toys these days!)

A cacophony of eldritch sounds, unsoothing to elderly ears, shatters the normal quiet of my home, and I love it Not the loudness, of course, but the fact is that there is young life about, so I'll put up with a lot. Parents of today must remember that it won't last, and they, too, may have a quiet house one day.

'Ah', I hear you say, 'She only gets the row at weekends. We have it every day!' We grandmas are a different case, of course, and, like the three wise monkeys, we learn that it is certainly expedient to see all, hear all, and say nowt, especially not to mothers and fathers who have the right to bring up their own progeny as they will. We have to remember how we resented any interference regarding our own children.

That being said, and tending as I do to compare the idols of today's children with those of my own youth in the early thirties, I recall that we, too, had mad pashes on crooners, dance-band leaders and film stars of the silent silver screen. We would cut out pictures from magazines and treasure them, just as children now buy very expensive posters to adorn their rooms. We would idolise the then Prince of Wales, who was never crowned king, and drool over the painting of the long-dead poet Lord Byron, just because there was a romantic picture of him wearing an Albanian turban.

But at least then men looked like men then, and not wimpish or androgenous. There I go again; we grannies must not be po-faced or even po-voiced. We would even have pashes (short for passions) on our teachers, who would be female in a girls' grammar school. Nothing was thought of this, for nothing was intended. Innocence was all, but today, and frightening to think of, other motives might be suggested. It is nicer to forget such modern thinking, and better to remember how we saved up our pocket money, or even some of our meagre wages, for at 14 many were working.

To see and hear Harry Roy playing 'Tiger Rag' was something never to be forgotten. The boys of the band, all in dress suits, would stand and sit in unison as they played the rousing song of the times. 'HOLD that tiger' the trumpets and saxophones roared, in very imitation of a great tiger.

The high notes rose to where the magical mirrored witch-bowls hung from dance-hall ceilings. The boys were musicians to a man. The cost of seeing a performance of Lew Stone's band, with the gorgeous Al Bowlly crooning 'The Very Thought of You', was 2s. 6d. (12½p). How many old hearts will beat a little faster remembering those velvet tones? Romance was romance then, or was it just because we had that precious gift of youth?

Al Bowlly was my idol and folk were heartbroken when he was killed by a land-mine during the war. My adoration had waned a bit by then because of an incident on a holiday. I approached him, autograph book at the ready, at a dance hall in the Isle of Man. He smiled rather haughtily and obliged some pretty women with his signature. I was a skinny, short-socked teenager adoring him as he strolled along the circle of the theatre in the interval. To be ignored hurt a lot. He didn't know, of course, how I would spend hours with my ear pressed to our faulty loudspeaker of our home-made wireless in our kitchen, just to hear his enchanting voice. Every word of 'Love Walked Right In' would be scribbled down, to by mulled over later.

He will be remembered while we oldies last. Will today's pop stars, who gyrate and spin about our stages under strobe-lighting, have near-immortality? I am sure my grandchildren will think so, for they are brain-washed by advertising and publicity even to buy the drinks THEY drink and emulate THEIR dress in every tiny detail. But wait, didn't we in days gone by make ourselves hats just like the Princess Marina's when she first delighted our eyes? Didn't our mothers, who were modern then, paint their lips like those of Clara Bow? Didn't we wear our hair over one eye like Veronica Lake?

How many grandfathers of today wore spats and double-breasted waistcoats emulating Adolph Menjou, that 1920s follower of fashion? In my girlhood, an older relation thought her husband was like Rudolph Valentino, so he tried to look sleepy-eyed, mysterious and sulky. His hair was like patent-leather, and he cultivated side-boards.

How many Oldhamers would journey to Manchester in the old days to see Victor Sylvester and his wife dance with style and elegance or experiment with the new blues to songs like 'Charmaine' or 'Blue Skies'? That really was music for romance — not like 'Let's Spend the Night Together' music of today.

Remembering how we, too, could be fanatical about our idols, I appreciate the youngsters' views and am tolerant. But often I have to referee when one idolises a spotty, ear-ringed and spike-haired singer and another adores a prancing, bewigged, crotch-hugging-trousered, microphone-up-the-nostril balladeer. My youngest grandchild, shut in her sister's room and in a temper, tore from the wall a treasured poster of the gesticulating big-eyed Jackson. She took the Michael, as it were.

Grandparents who would not wish long-gone idols to be mocked must be careful not to mock theirs —not if we like to co-exist peacefully, that is. There really are times when discretion is the better part of valour.

★ ★ ★ ★ ★

I learned, when I lived in Oldham, that people were very witty and, as they say, 'Had all their chairs at home'. I might have known that their teenagers of today, in common with teenagers all over the country, have a few sofas as well.

Recently, on a Manchester-to-Oldham train, I asked for it, to coin a phrase. Most people will find as they get older that they have to take care that they don't become invisible. There was a time when the proper place for grandmothers and grandfathers was deemed to be the chimney corner, alongside the hob and the great black iron kettle.

Grandmas were handy for poking the fire, rattling the poker on the chimney back when neighbours became noisy. Grandfathers smoked their pipes of peace and spat in the fire or, if their aim was poor, on the sleeping cat on the rag rug, or their brown spittle bubbled and hissed loudly on the bars of the fire.

Times are different now, and we silver tops have found our voices, but must take care not to be too strident and antagonise the young, who, perhaps to the surprise of some, have a lovely sense of humour and very quick wits. The choice for us, therefore, is either to be too accommodating and uncritical, in other words to lean over backwards not to offend, or to do as so many older people do and be overcritical and antagonistic. There are no training schools for oldies, and certainly none for grandparents. I sometimes wish there were.

For grannies who may read this, there is a lovely poem by Jenny Joseph about her intention of growing old gracefully — how she will learn to spit, and to wear purple, with a red hat that does not match. She intends to 'run her stick along the public railings, wear satin sandals, spend her money on brandy and summer gloves'. She will make up for the sobriety of her youth besides 'learning to spit'. I suppose in a way she is almost echoing what Dylan Thomas said about going not gentle into that good night, but urging to 'Rage, rage, against the dying of the light'. Put more bluntly, if less poetically, we must not be put on as we get older or swim with the tide, for sometimes tides can wash you away. But, just as important, we grandparents must not put upon the young by interfering with their lives or their own parents' ideas of bringing up their own young. A fine balance is very difficult to achieve, as so many of us learn by experience.

As one who remembers her granny as a little old woman in black jet-trimmed bonnet, with little button boots and a sealskin cape, you can tell I'm a granny in the older age bracket.

Grandma was respected, though, and coming back to today, we all must take care how we interact with youths. It was a lesson I had obviously not learned well, as I found to my cost on the Manchester-Oldham train. I should have known better.

The train was an ancient corridor type, with brass fittings, shabby plush upholstery and with a luggage rack which looked to be made out of string. It smelled of ancient dust and defunct mice, but when I commented to the BR man with his walkie-talkie that it looked antique, he told be brusquely that I didn't need to get on it. That should have warned me about keeping quiet.

I settled down in my corner of a compartment on this old corridor train. It was packed. It was a non-smoker, and a group of young boys filled the rest of the carriage. They started to smoke and, just recovering from an illness which had turned me canary-coloured, I was feeling, to say the least, rather jaundiced, and pointed out that the carriage was a non-smoker. They politely put out their fags, I said 'Thank you', they said 'Pleasure'. We rattled along towards Oldham

I was just complimenting myself on this outcome when they started talking about the decrepit train ... how it was like the Orient Express. They invented a clever scenario about a murder in the toilet. (Well, bog, they said!) I tried not to laugh as their inventive powers took over, but they were very clever lads and full of northern wit. I must point out that I was wearing my Cheshire hat, which is rather like a shallow chamber pot and clamped on my head only on windy days.

As the boys developed their theme and the solving of the plot, one of them said 'It's all right, lads, we've got Miss Marple with us'. Game, set and match, I thought, as the teenagers disembarked in Oldham. As I said, I should have known better.

Skeleton in the Cupboard

A hall which has disappeared, the Saint John Ambulance Hall in Chapel Walk, Preston, is no more. There are two slim pillars set in a wall there — could they be remnants of it, I wonder? There in the twenties, as children, some of us played with Agnes, the skeleton in the cupboard. She was a true bone skeleton, not like the plastic ones used today in medical schools.

There are probably other pensioners who lived in Preston in the twenties who also made a companion of her. I say 'her' because we called her Agnes, and she lived where skeletons are supposed to live ... in a cupboard. She must have had the requisite bone structure to indicate she had been a woman. My dad said she was probably a pauper in life, which is a terrible word, upsetting to the ear and the conscience. So we children of that age pitied her and were not in the least afraid. Her fixed grin was a happy one, her dangling arms and legs with the delicate feet could be made to dance to any song we chose to sing. It might be 'Life is Just A Bowl Of Cherries' or that terrible ditty of 1926 or so ... 'Ain't it grand to be blooming well dead!' A more appropriate song, 'Dem Bones, Dem Bones, Dem Dry Bones,' was perhaps not around then. We daren't sing the dreadful second song at home, for fear of a clip around the ear. But when the group of children opened up Agnes's long brown cupboard there were no adults around. They were all occupied in the Ambulance Hall, just off Fishergate, playing whist; entrance fee, one shilling.

The ones who ran the whist drives allowed parents to take children along, and we played on the first floor of the Ambulance Hall, whilst the card players used the ground floor.

Just as bingo players go out for an evening's gaming, with the hope of winning a bit of money, so did those whist players of the twenties hope to win prizes. There would be Westminster chiming clocks, canteens of cutlery, cut-glass vases and even a small booby prize for one with the lowest score. Mother and Father both played whist, and had also been members of the St. John Ambulance Brigade, so I spent many happy hours playing with Agnes, and with other children. We practised using the triangular bandages and splints, trying to make sense of the many charts on the walls in that upstairs room. Agnes, of course, was the skeleton used in teaching the Ambulance men — and women.

So the whist drives were a pleasant night out for working folk of the times, and a little family occasion. The hall was warm and smelled of hot-water pipes and the aroma of strong tea being brewed at the interval. Ladies wore their hats as they played at the green baize-covered tables; the men would leave their trilby hats and black bowlers in the cloakroom. They smoked their pipes and cigarettes with their cups of tea — not many ladies smoked in public then. Sometimes someone would play the piano and the whole atmosphere was one of friendliness. We children would be given biscuits and milk before dashing back upstairs to spend more time with Agnes.

What simple pleasures for adults and children alike. We made 'slides' on the polished floor, wearing out our cycle stockings, and we left the door of Agnes's cupboard open so she could watch the fun, perhaps more fun than she had enjoyed in her poverty-stricken life.

Then when it was time to go home, we tidied everything away, and carefully fastened the long brown cupboard door with its little hook, after telling Agnes that we would see her next week.

Then home along Fishergate, with its clanking trams. Or we might, for a change, go through leafy Winckley Square, with its elegant houses with their lovely front doors. Dad said some of the doors were Georgian, and they had little iron boot-scrapers on the steps. The steps seemed to be of a special kind of stone, all smooth and so different from our rough 'donkey-stoned' front step. There were iron railings all around the gardens then; they were removed to aid the war effort later on. There was a great horse chestnut tree at the top corner of Winckley Square, opposite the Junior Park School, and an owl hooted in the branches sometimes. If Dad had won a prize and was in expansive mood, we would call at Sandham's chip shop in Avenham Lane for two two's and a fish. A family night out was over, and with any luck we would be in time to hear A. J. Allen telling a story on our home-made wireless set. Nights to remember ... with delight.

The Phantom

Sixty years ago, the Phantom of the Opera scared the living daylights out of me, so much so that I had to have a nightlight for several months. Grown women fainted when watching the silent film of that name, which was showing in a dusty Preston picture-house in 1926; I was only a child of eight. The star was Lon Chaney. When his mutilated unmasked face, chalky as a death's head, loomed out of the flickering screen, strong men quaked and my childish self was petrified with fear. I doubt if I would be brave enough, even now, to go to the fabulous musical should it ever come to Manchester ... I think the trauma of long ago would still be with me, and I fear I would hide my face in my hands at the crucial moment.

Recently, seeing on television the glittering razzmatazz as the Duchess of York attended the Broadway show of the 'Phantom of the Opera', my mind went back to 1926 and the memory of my frightening, never to be forgotten, experience, and the winter's night was before my mind's eye as clearly as if it were yesterday. To paraphrase a famous quotation, I thought to myself ... 'How very different is the life and experience of our own dear duchess from that of the Lancashire lass of so long ago'.

I had never been to the pictures before, and as we went up the cobbled street, which was lighted by gas-lamps, I was so excited I skipped along, my hand tightly held by Father. Mother thought pictures were just a little bit sinful, and as a Baptist she was not too keen to go to the King's Palace. I know that I was eight years old, because I was wearing my yellow woollen gauntlet gloves, which I liked to wear with my Brownie uniform, because they matched the Brownie tie (so that dates my experience) and I can remember so well the feel of my gloved hand in Father's ... so very long ago! My brother, who was eighteen, had enjoyed the film and recommended it; he can't have realised how frightened I would be, and we left him at home fiddling with the home-made wireless set, twiddling the knobs to get Daventry and 2LO, no doubt glad to get us out of the way so that he could pursue his hobby and loop even more wires around our kitchen.

We had to queue under the cinema's grimy glass canopy before the doors opened for the first house. Our seats were tip-up balding velvet ones, with wooden arm-rests, and the floor was linoleum-covered, but the little place smelled nice. This was because the usherettes sprayed scent about, probably to cover the smell of wet clothes which were often made of 'shoddy', which gave off a pungent odour when damp. Folk did not bathe as much then, so the masking perfume served its purpose well. Some of the Woodbine cigarettes and tobacco from the men's pipes caused quite a fug, too, and often the screen was seen through a bluish haze of smoke.

Unfortunately, I saw the film only too clearly on that occasion, though I quite liked the beginning of the picture, with the Opera House scenes and the pretty silent screen star, whose name I don't remember. I began to be frightened when she was carried away into the bowels of the building after the appearance of the Phantom, in brimmed hat and flowing cape, gliding along the great rafters above the Opera House's immense chandelier. When the heroine was showered with gifts and ensconced in a great silk-bedecked bed, I almost pitied the Phantom just as I had pitied the Beast in 'Beauty and the Beast'. Such devotion almost seemed wonderful to my mind. I was not too severely frightened at first, for the Phantom wore his mask at all times. He warned the beautiful lady never to touch this and she, like me, and the watchers of this silent film, was not to know what horror remained to be seen.

Then came the moment which is etched so deeply on my mind. The Phantom was playing at an organ, the beautiful woman crept up, silently, behind him ... and with one movement whipped the concealing mask from the terrible face!

The hollow eyes, the nose like two holes in the face, the skull like a death's head was revealed. We saw the 'silent scream' as the creature opened his mouth with the blackened teeth; his anger was terrible to see! A great gasp arose from the audience. The ghastly face seemed to enlarge and come towards me, and I was terrified. Later, the Phantom walked under the waters of an underground lake, breathing through an iron tube, and that scene, too, is still with me. It seemed so very sinister, that this horrible creature was actually walking below water, and sixty years on I see the scene still.

My parents had to provide me with a light at night for many months, so dreadful was the memory of the frightful face. Today's children, used as they are to frightening pictures on television, would surely take the old film of the Phantom of the Opera in their stride. But yesterday, even to see Michael Crawford, with his white plastic mask, on television, caused a shudder of remembered fear to trouble me even now. I'll remember the Phantom of the Opera as long as I live!

Magic!

Of all the things which happened in my young life, nothing can compare with the magic, the sheer magic, of hearing voices out of the air for the very first time. The wireless, for ordinary folk, was new to us in the twenties when I was a little girl.

My older brother and my father worked hard assembling cats' whiskers sets with the aid of a magazine about wireless construction. They built sets using small sheets of bakelite and things called oscillators and condensors, and some fascinating stuff called Flux, a dark yellowy grease which, I recall, had the property of making silvery solder. Our little gas jet in the kitchen was always alight for the soldering iron. Fragile opalescent valves had to be handled carefully and there came high screechings and demon wailings from our little set as Dad and my brother twiddled knobs. They would splice wires which seemed to be looped all over the picture-rails when later we had the addition of home-made loud-speakers perched high on the walls. The wires almost obliterated the large prints of 'The Boyhood of Raleigh' and 'Between Two Fires' (pictures obtained from cigarette coupons from the Gold Flake cigarettes Dad smoked in dozens as he hopefully searched for 2L.O. or Daventry!). I never could understand why the new magic was named 'wireless' when there seemed to be yards of the stuff festooning our kitchen.

We only had one pair of headphones at first, so one half would be removed and I would have to clamp the half to my ear whilst Dad had the half with the head-band — all agog with anticipation and straining for the first magical sounds. The little sets were powered (if that's the right word) by accumulators which were like heavy glass boxes, filled with acid. They each had a carrying handle, for they had to be charged at regular intervals. You could always tell an accumulator-carrying man or woman — their trouser-bottoms or skirts had holes burned in them from the spilled acid.

Unforgettable was the thrill, the absolute rapture of hearing a soprano from Savoy Hill. Father explained that the singing was from hundreds of miles away, that it travelled through the very air to our Preston kitchen, and the truth was almost unbelievable, and magnificent! When the song ended, there was a puzzling sound, almost like heavy rain falling on the roof ... what could it be? People clapping their hands, Mother explained, applauding ... in a studio, in a big city. Wonderful!

With the added advantage of the loudspeakers, home-made, with their fret-worked plywood fronts, the voices, songs, stories and plays could be heard all over the kitchen, without the need for headphones. A new era was upon us. Home entertainment, to replace the dominoes, the cards, the crossword puzzles (new then), the piano-playing.

A good story-teller on the wireless could make you see a picture of all he said. There was a man called A. J. Allen whose mellifluous voice could have charmed snakes. I can, today, remember his story of 'The Monkey's Paw' by E. W. Jacobs. This was a thriller and terrifying when heard late at night when a small child should have been in bed. It is a tale of a family who were given a monkey's paw which had the power to grant three wishes. With the second wish the mother asks for her dead son to return from the grave. She makes her wish, and they all wait — in silence. I sat on our kitchen table, knees clasped to my chest, head strained upwards in order to get a little closer to our home-made speaker positioned near the picture-rail ... still silence ... we wait ... breath baited, heart hammering. And then ... when the suspense is becoming unbearable ... then, in the home of the family, and coming nearer and nearer, ever closer — the sound of dragging footsteps ... they get close to the door of the home ... then the slow, loud knocking on the door — one, two, three. The dead son has returned, terror was in my heart as I waited for the mother to open the door ... what horror would confront her? Horror and dreadful anticipation gripped my being as I waited and suffered with the bereaved mother. No moment of dramatic theatre or television has superseded that moment in 1926 or thereabouts — I doubt if it ever will — my mind was young and like wax then, imprinting the memories, the lasting memories.

Children's Hour, at tea-time each day, was eagerly awaited. In imagination I walked the country lanes with Romany and Aunties Doris and Vi. I could almost see, no, not almost, I could see the dog which bounded along with them, being called to heel as he frightened a poor hedgehog into a prickly ball ... and I almost lifted my feet up in imitation of the Aunties as they were told to 'Watch out for the puddles' in the lane ... simple stuff, but magical. There was a spot in the programme when the Aunts gave out birthday greetings to kids whose parents had written in, and instructions were given out over the air as to where hidden birthday presents could be found ... 'Look in Daddy's bureau, Ronald' ... or 'Search under the lid of Mummy's piano, Cynthia!' What on earth was a Bureau? ... all the kids seemed to have them in their homes, it seemed, in the twenties ... but not in ours, of course. Simple stuff, but pure magic then.

When Eric Fogg (Uncle Eric) lost his life beneath an underground train, we children who listened to Children's Hour truly felt we had lost a real uncle.

Another source of wonder was the gramophone. We didn't have such a luxury, but my small Scottish friend did. We would be invited into their tiny parlour in Frenchwood, Preston, with its horsehair sofa and shiny linoleum and treated to records (sixpence from Woolworth's) of Will Fyffe or Harry Lauder.

Sometimes we had the only English record they owned, one of a rumbustious comic called Billy Bennett, whose naughty line in one monologue was about a lady who 'went out and married a darkie — and so for her sins she got three sets of twins — one black — one white — and one khaki!' VERY risqué, that, in the days when one comedian was banned from the wireless for mentioning that a lady's waist-line might alter from one month to the next.

So there we would sit, three skinny children and one plump one, our behinds cold from the lino, no fires in parlours unless it was Sunday, the sun filtering weakly through the lace curtains, luxuriating in the magic of hearing the tinny-sounding voices issuing from the big green horn of the gramophone. We took turns in winding the handle when the mechanism ran down, and we sat for hours listening to the songs sung in accents as thick as porridge.

The magic of the Twenties would seem dull indeed to our young children of today. They take for granted the advent of television, computers and video recorders — as well as the horrors of Exocet missiles and moon-shots.

But my 'magic' of so long ago is for ever.